NARRATIVES
of SOCIAL *and* ECONOMIC JUSTICE

ROBERTA R. GREENE
HARRIET L. COHEN
JOHN GONZALEZ
and YOUJUNG LEE

NASW PRESS

NATIONAL ASSOCIATION OF SOCIAL WORKERS

Washington, DC

James J. Kelly, PhD, ACSW, LCSW, *President*

Elizabeth J. Clark, PhD, ACSW, MPH, *Executive Director*

Cheryl Y. Bradley, *Publisher*
Lisa M. O'Hearn, *Managing Editor*
John Cassels, *Project Manager and Staff Editor*
Patrice Pascual, *Copyeditor*
Linda Elliot, *Proofreader*
Karen Schmitt, *Indexer*

Cover by Ellipse Design, a Division of Balmar, Inc.
Interior design by Ellipse Design, a Division of Balmar, Inc.
Printed and bound by Port City Press

Library of Congress Cataloging-in-Publication Data

Narratives of social and economic justice / Roberta R. Greene . . . [et al.].
    p. cm.
  Includes bibliographical references and index.
  ISBN 978-0-87101-388-0
  1. Age discrimination—United States—Case studies. 2. Social justice—United States—Case studies. I. Greene, Roberta R. (Roberta Rubin), 1940–
  HQ1064.U5N22 2009
  303.3'7209730904—dc22   2009027366

TABLE *of* CONTENTS

About the Authors

Roberta R. Greene, PhD, MSW, is professor and Louis and Ann Wolens Centennial Chair in Gerontology at the School of Social Work, University of Texas at Austin. Dr. Greene is the author and coauthor of numerous publications, including *Foundations of Social Work Practice in the Field of Aging: A Competency-Based Approach* (NASW Press, 2007), *Social Work Practice: A Risk and Resilience Perspective* (Brooks/Cole, 2007), *Contemporary Issues of Care* (Haworth Press, 2007), *Resiliency: An Integrated Framework for Practice, Research, and Policy* (NASW Press, 2002), and *Social Work with the Aged and Their Families* (Aldine de Gruyter, 2000). She serves on a number of editorial review boards, including that of the *Journal of Social Work Education,* and is currently engaged in research that incorporates filmmaking and Web site design.

Harriet L. Cohen, PhD, LCSW, is associate professor in the Department of Social Work, Texas Christian University (TCU) in Fort Worth, and brings 26 years of experience as a social work practitioner with older adults into the classroom and her research. She has published in numerous journals and is a coauthor of *Foundations of Social Work Practice in the Field of Aging: A Competency-Based Approach* (NASW Press, 2007). Since joining the faculty at TCU, Dr. Cohen has helped to establish the Center on Healthy Aging and to develop the Healthy Aging minor. Her research interests include two vulnerable populations—older Holocaust survivors and older lesbians and gay men—and her current research documents the contributions of Holocaust survivors in Texas, utilizing multimodal learning formats.

John M. Gonzalez, PhD, MSW, is assistant professor in the Department of Social Work, University of Texas–Pan American. Dr. Gonzalez received his BA in psychology and sociology from the University of Texas at Austin, his MSW from Texas State University at San Marcos, and his PhD from the University of Texas at Austin. A former Council on Social Work Education Minority Research Fellow, he has authored and coauthored a variety of publications on older Latinos and mental health services and older adults overcoming oppression. His research interests are older Latinos and the delivery of mental health services.

Youjung Lee, PhD, MSW, is visiting assistant professor, Department of Social Work, Binghamton University, State University of New York. Dr. Lee received her MSW in 2002 and her PhD in 2007 from the University of Texas at Austin. Her research interests involve positive aspect of family caregiving and resilience in minority older adults, focusing on the disparities of minority family caregiving dynamics between spouse caregivers and child caregivers. She has published on issues of minority family caregiving and the resilience of minority older adults who overcame discriminations and has taught on human behavior and the social environment and program evaluation in social work practice.

Dedication and Acknowledgements

We dedicate this book to the older adults who participated in the taping project *Older Adults Who Have Overcome Oppression*. Their stories teach us how personal fortitude, positive social support, and activism enabled them to transcend what could have been the debilitating effects of bigotry and prejudice.

We acknowledge Margaret Evans, who conducted some of the initial interviews, and Sandra Graham for her figure depicting the four levels of the narrative.

INTRODUCTION

NARRATIVES OF SOCIAL AND ECONOMIC JUSTICE: A COMPETENCY-BASED APPROACH

A Research Project

The narratives for this work were collected during a research project that explored the factors that enabled selected older adults to overcome early discrimination and become resilient adults. *Resilience* is a term that describes unpredicted or distinctly successful adaptations to negative life events, trauma, stress, or risk. A snowball sample obtained from social work practitioners and educators identified "successful" older adults respected for their work in overcoming discrimination and advocating for social justice. Researchers conducted semi-structured interviews to discover the personal characteristics and environmental factors that enabled the older adults to overcome negative life events (see Table 1).

Competency-Based Education

This text is organized around a competency-based approach to social work education. The competency-based approach to education, recently adopted by the Council on Social Work Education (see Table 2), "is an outcome performance approach to curriculum design" (Council on Social Work Education, 2008, p. 3). This means that upon graduation students are expected to demonstrate that they have mastered "measurable practice behaviors that are comprised of knowledge, values, and skills" (p. 3).

Each chapter presents core competencies and study questions and activities to measure mastery of chapter content. There is an emphasis on the reader's ability to

❖ apply critical thinking to inform and communicate professional judgments,

❖ understand how diversity characterizes and shapes the human experience and is critical to the formation of identity,

❖ understand the forms and mechanisms of oppression and discrimination, and

❖ recognize the interconnections of oppression and be knowledgeable about theories of social and economic justice.

Narratives of Social Justice

The text uses narrative accounts of 11 older men and women as vehicles for learning about the "interconnections of oppression" and the potential of "theories of justice and strategies to promote human and civil rights" (Council on Social Work Education, 2008, p. 5). It focuses

---

Table 1: Cultural Narrative: Open-Ended Interview Questions

1. Where did you grow up?

2. What was it like to be a child growing up there?

3. Was there much racism or discrimination?

4. What are some of the things that were done in your community that made you or your friends feel discriminated against?

5. How did people get around these threats or overcome hassles?

6. Whom did you know who really coped well or got around bad situations?

7. What made them good at bouncing back?

8. Was there someone who was particularly "good" at bouncing back?

9. What about you?

10. What types of help did people need or want when things got bad?

11. What did your family do to raise children (who felt "good" about being Black, Latino) when there was discrimination?

12. Did you teach your children ideas/strategies to prepare them for "bad things that might happen"?

13. Did they learn things about how to succeed?

14. How would you say you influenced your children or other young people in the community?

15. Did you tell them any stories?

16. What about the neighbors and community?

17. What should I write about for social work students to learn?

18. Did I miss some questions you would like to tell me?

---

on how the storytellers overcame discrimination based on ethnicity/race, religion, economic status, gender, or national origin. This book uses selected quotes from narratives to help the reader understand the social injustices of the Jim Crow era and how the storytellers maintained a resilient self and fostered a resilient family and community.

Each chapter is organized around the personal, interpersonal, sociocultural, and structural aspects of the narrative, leading to an understanding of the factors that enhanced the storytellers' resilience. From this perspective, personal narratives also represent a global sociocultural, historical, and political context, and may be thought of as stories about a given society at a particular point in time. Thus, the narratives

❖ provide insights about the historical context in which the storytellers lived,

❖ outline the nature of the "differences" that limited their equal participation in society,

---

Table 2: Council on Social Work Education *Educational Policy Statement*

❖ Educational Policy 2.1.1—Identify as a professional social worker and conduct oneself accordingly.

❖ Educational Policy 2.1.2—Apply social work ethical principles to guide professional practice.

❖ Educational Policy 2.1.3—Apply critical thinking to inform and communicate professional judgments.

❖ Educational Policy 2.1.4—Engage diversity and difference in practice.

❖ Educational Policy 2.1.5—Advance human rights and social and economic justice.

❖ Educational Policy 2.1.6—Engage in research-informed practice and practice-informed research.

❖ Educational Policy 2.1.7—Apply knowledge of human behavior and the social environment.

❖ Educational Policy 2.1.8—Engage in policy practice to advance social and economic well-being and to deliver effective social work services.

❖ Educational Policy 2.1.9—Respond to contexts that shape practice.

❖ Educational Policy 2.1.10(a)–(d)—Engage, assess, intervene, and evaluate with individuals, families, groups, organizations, and communities.

Source: Council on Social Work Education. (2008). *Educational policy and accreditation standards.* Alexandria, VA: Author.

❖ examine how the power relationships of the day affected their interpersonal relationships and societal rights and responsibilities,

❖ describe personal and environmental risk factors that may have interrupted the development of resilient personalities, families, and communities,

❖ discuss the legal barriers and social and economic injustices that needed to be overcome as the storytellers adapted to and engaged in civic responsibility,

❖ analyze how they negotiated power relationships to overcome the risks of discrimination, and

❖ describe actions taken at the personal, interpersonal, sociocultural, and structural levels that enabled the storytellers to be agents of change.

Each chapter also offers historical accounts and policy information to align the reader with each storyteller's personal context "across space and time" (Shuman, 2006, p. 152). This will help the reader understand how historic and current structures of social policies and services advance social and economic well-being (Council on Social Work Education, 2008). Our intent is to illustrate, through personal examples, that an individual's experience is part of collective memory, public discourse, and political identities (Shuman, 2006). Each chapter of the book presents an older adult's critical life events and describes how earlier conflict was reconciled (Coleman, 1999). Through this, the reader will learn what it was like when this older generation was growing up, and the lessons learned will provide an intergenerational cultural perspective on life events (Greene, 2007).

Definitions of social and economic justice provide additional means of understanding narrative accounts, as does an examination of societal power dynamics. Narratives bring to light how these older adults advocated for social justice; what allowed them to lead full, productive, and resilient lives; and how they left their mark on their family, community, and society. The reader will therefore develop an appreciation of how personal resilience is intertwined with social justice.

The text uses the ecological systems perspective to describe the complex transactions between people and their environments. Ecological thinking focuses on the multiple systems of influence in which people live. This approach contributes to the reader's understanding of the interplay of a person's particular life story with collective histories. That is, an individual's story, told in that person's own words, can "uncover how life reflects cultural themes of the society, personal themes, institutional themes, and social histories" (Creswell, 1998, p. 49).

As the narratives reveal, the stories of older adults can also express negative experiences "in which cultural meanings are subjugated" (Saleebey, 1994, p. 38). One reads their accounts to learn about their adaptations and strategies that ultimately led to a resilient sense of self, allowing them to overcome critical life events and challenges. The individual life stories also contribute to a collective understanding of the historical era that culminated in the Civil Rights movement of the 1960s.

As readers learn how the storytellers overcame societal injustice, they understand why promoting social and economic justice is a core social work value. Thus, "the teller not only recovers her voice; she becomes a witness to the conditions that rob others of their voices. When any person recovers his voice, many people begin to speak through history" (Frank, cited in Shuman, 2006, p. 153).

Chapter Content

Chapter 1 presents the historical background of the narrative form and introduces the reader to the four dimensions of storytelling. Chapter 2 discusses the issues of social and economic justice described by the storytellers. Definitions of social and economic justice are provided and examples are taken from the narratives to illustrate various types of discrimination.

Chapter 3 introduces the assumptions of risk and resilience theory, allowing the reader to understand the formation of the resilient self, family, and community. The term *resilience* refers to self-righting behavior with unpredicted or distinctly successful adaptations to negative life events, trauma, stress, or risk. Resilient people draw on internal resources, including hope and determination, as well as on external supports, such as mutual aid networks (Greene, 2002). Resilience is a "universal capacity which allows a person, group or community to prevent, minimize or overcome the damaging effects of adversity. Resiliency may transform or make stronger the lives of those who are resilient" (Grotberg, 1995).

Chapter 4 contains the first narrative, using the life of AS to illustrate the four levels of the narrative: personal, interpersonal, sociocultural, and societal/structural. Kenyon and Randall's (2001) four interrelated dimensions of life stories are adapted to categorize resilience: (a) the societal/*structural* encompasses social policies, power relations, and economic conditions; (b) the *sociocultural* refers to social meanings associated with aging and the life course; (c) the *interpersonal* includes interactions with families and friends; and (d) the *personal* involves internal meaning and coherence.

AS grew up with a single parent and a close extended family, including grandparents who provided unconditional love. His neighborhood was integrated but his one-room school, which he started attending at age four, was segregated. His mother moved the family to a larger town when AS was in eighth grade so he could continue higher levels of schooling. There, he discovered that there was a "Mexican school, a white school, and a black school." AS continued his education in a segregated school and upon graduation became the first black student at the University of Texas at Austin School of Social Work. During his career as a social worker, he worked as a counselor at a family service agency, founded a bank, and helped establish a housing complex with support from the U.S. Department of Housing and Urban Development.

In chapter 5, the descendents of families who lived in a once-thriving neighborhood describe school discrimination and the educational inequities they experienced while growing up. Quakertown was a middle-class African American community in Denton, Texas, from the mid-1870s through the early 1920s. It was probably named for the Quakers who helped the freedmen during Reconstruction. During the 1880s, schools, churches, businesses, and civic organizations were built in Quakertown to support the growing number of black residents.

In the early 1920s, the trustees of what is now Texas Women's University decided that they did not want their white daughters walking past a black neighborhood. The Denton City Commission issued a bond to purchase, demolish, or move Quakertown properties. Some residents sold their homes or moved them to Solomon Hill, currently part of southeast Denton, on the other side of the railroad tracks. The community of Quakertown was destroyed and the property adjacent to the campus of Texas Women's University is now the home of the city park.

Chapter 6 presents the life of JM, who grew up in Hampton, Virginia, which was then a segregated town of about 5,000 people. JM's story illustrates the importance of education as a vehicle for overcoming discrimination. Hampton is home to the Hampton Institute, one of the first historically black colleges in the United States. Though segregated, the town had a community of "solidly middle-class blacks," JM recalls. Other black residents were poor and worked as crab fishermen. Still, black employees who worked at nearby military bases were forced by law to ride in the back of the bus. JM, who worked on a military base after the school day ended, remembers being "persuaded" to move back to avoid trouble. Such experiences helped him to decide consciously to become part of the professional class.

JM received his MSW from a school in the South that had to send him north to complete his field practicum. He joined the military when the armed forces were still segregated. He later took advantage of opportunities provided by the military to get his doctorate. He rose to the rank of colonel in the Air Force and head of its social services, overseeing staff and acting on promotions.

Chapter 7, authored by John Gonzalez, discusses the life of GG, who overcame discrimination to become an educator. Issues of Spanish as a second language are discussed: Speaking Spanish was not allowed, and children were held back (not promoted).

GG was born in New Braunfels, Texas. He walked to a segregated school five or six miles from his home and did not speak English until he was 10 years old. He had attended 11 different schools before he dropped out at 17 and joined the Marine Corps. He remembers picking cotton and hoping to do more with his life.

In the Marines, GG was sent to a Japanese language school and recognized the value of an education. He got his general equivalency diploma and, following military service in Korea, earned a master's degree and a doctorate in education. He has been married for more than 50 years and four of his five children are college graduates. GG, who takes pride in his Latino heritage, has been a principal and a superintendent of education, and has an alternative high school named for him in Austin, Texas.

Chapter 8, authored by Youjung Lee, describes the life of JS, a successful Korean businessman who immigrated to the United States to establish an export–import business.

To accomplish his "American dream," he had to overcome housing and other forms of discrimination.

Chapter 9, written by Harriet L. Cohen, presents the life of JG, a Jewish woman living in the South but originally from New York. Her story exemplifies the making of an activist. JG did not experience discrimination until she married and moved to Mississippi with her husband in 1955. At that time, public schools were being integrated and JG was asked to join a group that favored racial segregation. She refused and instead helped to form the Panel of American Women, an advocacy group that fought discrimination and promoted school integration. Panel members toured Mississippi, making as many as 1,000 presentations. Such advocacy could be dangerous; JG remembers her synagogue and rabbi's house being bombed. Her family was ostracized for being pro-integrationists.

Finally, Chapter 10 examines the life of PC, a Catholic nun, activist, and role model. She describes how she listened to people's stories as a community organizer in *colonias*, very low-income areas of the Texas–Mexico border that may not have running water or sewers.

References

Coleman, P. G. (1999). Creating a life story: The task of reconciliation. *Gerontologist, 39,* 133–139.

Council on Social Work Education. (2008). *Educational policy and accreditation standards.* Alexandria, VA: Author.

Creswell, J. W. (1998). *Qualitative inquiry and research design: Choosing among five traditions.* Thousand Oaks, CA: Sage Publications.

Greene, R. R. (Ed.). (2002). *Resiliency: An integrated approach to practice, policy, and research.* Washington, DC: NASW Press.

Greene, R. R. (2007). *Social work practice: A risk and resilience perspective.* Monterey, CA: Brooks/Cole.

Grotberg, E. H. (1995, September). *The International Resilience Project: Research, application, and policy.* Paper presented at the Symposio International Stress e Violencia, Lisbon, Portugal.

Kenyon, G. M., & Randall, W. L. (2001). Narrative gerontology: An overview. In G. M. Kenyon, P. Clark, & B. de Vries (Eds.), *Narrative gerontology: Theory, research, and practice* (pp. 3–8). New York: Springer.

Saleebey, D. (1994). *The strengths perspective in social work practice.* Boston: Allyn & Bacon.

Shuman, A. (2006). Entitlement and empathy in personal narrative. *Narrative Inquiry, 16,* 148–155.

NARRATIVE GERONTOLOGY: FOUR DIMENSIONS

This chapter emphasizes the following competencies:

Students will

❖ use critical thinking to synthesize and communicate information;

❖ use research evidence to inform practice; and

❖ plan to engage in practices that advance social and economic justice.

The Narrative: A Scientific Approach

This chapter describes the various uses of the narrative and explains how a narrative may help supply research data and clinical information.

In the late 19th and early 20th centuries, researchers developed a scientific interest in life stories, emphasizing the link between *personality* (or enduring characteristics of the individual such as self-esteem) and *social structure* (or normative characteristics of social systems such as roles and norms) revealed in people's life stories (Ryff, Marshall, & Clarke, 1999). Social scientists then studied people's internal views of their lives and their relationship to the social view of the self (Cooley, 1902/1964; Mead, 1934).

Narrative gerontology developed during the late 20th century as a scientific approach to human development, a field of research that explores the lives of older adults through storytelling. As such, narrative gerontology offers a perspective or a way of gathering new insights on aging (Kenyon & Randall, 2001). The approach is now used in theory building, research, and practice.

One advantage of the narrative is that it is an expression of how people have functioned during their lives, providing the researcher with information or "data" about the aging process (Kenyon, Clark, & de Vries, 2001, p. xii). From this perspective, older adults' subjective memories may offer knowledge about the human condition and thus can be considered part of a qualitative approach to the scientific method.

Each person's story is deemed unique and is accepted at face value. Although the purpose of obtaining a narrative is to retain each person's "voice," when conducting a study a researcher may aggregate information from several life stories, putting the "pieces" together (Bluck, 2001). In this way, details drawn from several life stories may help readers to understand both the individual and the collective meaning of societal issues such as discrimination and oppression.

Narratives as Stories

In the simplest terms, a narrative is a story or the relating of events by one person to another (Birren, 2001). Stories encompass characters, plots, and themes. They are memories of past events, and meanings are attributed to them. Usually, storytellers describe the "best" and "worst" of times. They are able to place themselves in history, give meaning to past events and remembering and aspire to goals in the future, often imagining "future selves" (Markus & Nurius, 1986).

A *narrative*, then, is a story or a person's account of life events, an interpretation of how he or she has experienced life events. Sometimes the storyteller feels a sense of regret. We have chosen storytellers who have perceived positive outcomes despite the adversities of discrimination and oppression during their lifetimes. As we read their personal histories, we find out that they have righted old wrongs, reconciled with their "enemies," take pride in their accomplishments, and feel that they have done their best. The accounts of their lives also provide us with knowledge and values useful for composing our own lives (Butler, 1968).

Constructing stories and interpreting their meaning is a universal human capacity (Birren, 2001). In fact, the process of telling one's life experiences to another is as old as history itself. This process, reflected in poems, drama, oral histories, and, of course, autobiographies, continues to provide people with cultural, social, historical, and recreational benefits.

Narratives as Culture and Social Systems

There are rich differences in people's experiences and the expression of their stories. This is because stories are influenced by the multiple social systems and cultures that affect human development (Webster, 2001). *Culture* is a way of life that binds a community together. It may be understood as "people's shared cognitive map, their discourse, and how they go about their lives—their life perspective" (Greene, 2002, p. 246). Because culture binds a community together and offers a set of norms and values, it has the potential to shape the storytelling process. Therefore, one can expect stories to reflect shared values, beliefs, and expectations of a given society (Webster, 2001) and the "collective thought process of a people or culture" (Cross, 1998, p. 144).

In this text, we use two conceptual frameworks to organize the various social systems described in the narratives. First, life stories are examined as the ecological systems in which people live. Ecological systems include small-scale *microsystems*, such as families and peer groups; midrange *mesosystems*, such as senior centers and the workplace; and *macrosystems*, or the legal and political systems that enact and administer policies affecting such things as discriminatory practices (Kirst-Ashman & Hull, 1993). Thus, the reader can understand social justice issues and resilience at each ecological level.

The second organizing framework used to explore the narratives is that of Kenyon and Randall (2001), who suggested that there are four dimensions of life stories (see Figure 1):

1. The *personal* dimension of narratives provides insights into the subjective world of the storytellers. It allows one to understand the inner meaning of their lives, contextualized in terms of culture, gender, class, and ethnicity (McAdams, 1996). In addition, the personal dimension demonstrates ways in which older adults achieved their own personal goals and exhibited strengths such as perseverance and determination.

2. The *interpersonal* dimension involves storytellers' relationships with family and peer groups. Their interpersonal accounts may include mentoring others, playing, and working with peers. For example, T., an African American woman, lovingly recalled her childhood in central Texas:

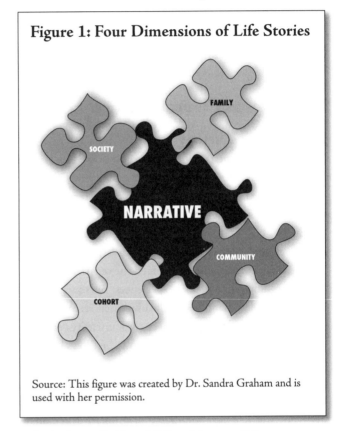

Figure 1: Four Dimensions of Life Stories

SOCIETY

FAMILY

NARRATIVE

COMMUNITY

COHORT

Source: This figure was created by Dr. Sandra Graham and is used with her permission.

> I know many a day when we would walk and come back home in the neighborhood where I was. We would find many things on the porch where somebody had come by and left things for us. So as you said we were poor, but everybody in the neighborhood where I lived was poor, but we didn't know it and we were happy. Our Spanish people and our white people, we played together—the children, the Spanish parents, the white parents would come and visit in our home. We had a piano, and a lot of people would like to come into our house to play the piano and sing and gather around. So as long as we stayed in the little area where we was, it was fine, and really the difference was the school situation uptown.

3. The *sociocultural* dimension encompasses the social meanings associated with aging within a particular social context, for instance the ways in which older adults con-

trast their generation with others. The older adult narratives in this text may refer to the Great Depression or World War II as being of their generation. In this respect, narratives or personal stories give insight into an individual's life-in-context, bringing one that much closer to understanding the complexities of lives in communities during a given time (Cole & Knowles, 2001).

4. The *structural* dimension is comparable to macrosystems and includes the social policies, power relations, and economic conditions of a given society. Structural dimensions of the featured narratives include such things as how older adults obtained housing, accessed education, and used transportation.

Narratives as Clinical Practice

Narratives as Therapy

Psychotherapists such as Sigmund Freud, Alfred Adler, and Carl Jung conceptualized avenues for recalling life events, suggesting that the process had remedial effects. That is, the psychotherapeutic techniques for listening to and interpreting a patient's autobiographical memory were viewed as a means of solving problems and changing behaviors (Birren, 2001).

In 1963, Robert Butler, a pioneer in geriatric psychiatry, first called attention to reminiscence as an adaptive function for older adults; he believed it could help them find new significance and meaning in their lives. He coined the term *life review* to describe the autobiographical process of recalling past personal experiences. Borrowing from Eriksonian theory (Erikson, 1963), Butler contended that older adults used their retrospective memories, particularly potent in old age, to resolve the developmental crisis of integrity versus despair in which one achieves wisdom and peace, thereby making sense of how their lives had changed over time.

Listening to reminiscence—"the progressive return to consciousness of past experiences, particularly the resurgence of unresolved conflicts" (Butler, 1968, p. 242)—has since become an important feature of mental health treatment and empirical research. The connection between psychological well-being and positive personality reorganization continues to be studied today (Arean et al., 1993; Greene, 2002; Webster & Haight, 2002). For example, Haight, Michel, and Hendrix (2000) conducted a study of reminiscence as an intervention to relieve depression among nursing home residents. They concluded that life review is indeed an effective time-limited intervention that has lasting effects on alleviating depression.

Narratives as Reconstruction

Obtaining narratives is facilitated by people's natural tendency to tell the stories of their lives, which reveal insights about personal and social functioning across the life course. A narrative differs from a life review, during which the social worker focuses mainly on intrapsychic issues. When obtaining a narrative, the practitioner is interested in exploring the historical and cultural meaning of events. In addition, when used as a form of therapy, the narrative interview offers older adults the opportunity to rethink, reconstruct, and celebrate their stories, perhaps transcending earlier adverse events (Greene, 2007).

According to McNamee and Gergen (1992) in their book *Therapy as Social Construction*, by taking "a not knowing stance," the therapist creates a space for client dialogue and lets the client's story emerge. There are no presuppositions about the "problem" and no "universal standards" by which human development is measured. Rather, development over the life span is highly variable and embodied in the client's story (Gergen & Gergen, 1983).

The narrative perspective dissolves the dichotomy between expert social worker and non-expert client often found in the medical model. Instead of describing a person as a "problem," the professional listens to the client's story and is instructed about the client's concerns. This process is sometimes called a *dialogic approach*, in which storytellers (patients/clients) and story readers (professional providers) become conversant with each other (Clark, 2001). In this way, the client is an active participant in the helping process (White & Epston, 1990).

Anderson and Goolishian (1992) summarized eight assumptions of narrative therapy:

1. Therapeutic systems are linguistic, a product of social communication (i.e., the social worker–client conversation).
2. Therapy is based on communication as a form of action. What will the client "make" of his or her life?
3. Through the therapeutic conversation, the problem is organized and "dissolved."
4. Therapy is based on the use of language, through which one generates new meaning.
5. The role of the therapist is participant–facilitator of the therapeutic conversation.
6. The therapist uses the art of therapeutic questions.
7. Problems center around issues that diminish clients' sense of agency or personal liberation.
8. Re-storying the problem offers a new sense of agency.

Narratives in Health Care

Health and human service providers are increasingly using a narrative approach to understand the aging process and later life. For example, the field of medicine generally uses language that embodies institutional categories, a distinct nomenclature, and descriptive protocols. Diagnoses and prognoses are a necessary part of its scientific inquiry. However, obtaining medical information through the use of narrative could encourage people to express the way they make sense of their own situation.

Clark (2001) suggested that physicians use a patient-centered clinical approach to medical practice, in which patients are encouraged to give their stories in their own voices rather than conform to technical language. He went on to quote Hunter, Charon, and Coulehan (1995), who suggested that

> clinical practice is founded on the stories that patients tell their doctors and that doctors translate into cases. Helping doctors and medical students to understand these stories and to grasp their significance is an important response to patients' most damning lament about health care—that their doctors do not listen to them. (p. 791)

Clark (2001) offered another example for occupational therapists about what can be gained from listening to client narratives. He suggested that a story that focuses on past work history can answer several questions:

❖ What activities and roles were important to this client before his or her illness?

❖ What valued activities and roles can this client perform now?

❖ What valued activities and roles are possible in the future, given his or her residual disability?

❖ What valued activities and roles would the client choose as priorities for the future? (pp. 199–200)

Narrative therapy has also received increased attention in teaching hospitals, conveying fuller meaning to views of illness, treatment choices, and treatment goals (Gass, 2001). Moreover, it is increasingly used by health professionals to understand a person's past and present life (Hallberg, 2001). In short,

> whatever our professional role—counselor, chaplain, caregiver, nurse—a narrative perspective explodes our sense of the person in front of us. She is not a patient, client, or case. She is not "the gall bladder in 13A" but a person with a story as rich as our own. . . . She is not an illustration of a statistical trend, but a unique aesthetic entity, a work of art that is one-of-a-kind. . . . A narrative perspective escorts us then to the "soul" of a person. (Randall, 2001, p. 47)

Narratives as Culturally Sound Social Work Practice

Listening to and acknowledging client narratives and meaning is a vehicle for enhancing culturally based social work practice, an important professional goal (see Table 3). Narrative interviewing has also been used in social work practice (Kropf & Tandy, 1998) to challenge existing assumptions—when culture comes to life but is also rewritten or takes on new meaning (Gubrium, 1993). According to the Council on Social Work Education (2008) *Educational Policy and Accreditation Standards*, students will engage diversity and difference in practice

> and understand how diversity characterizes and shapes the human experience and is critical to the formation of identity. The dimensions of diversity are understood as the intersectionality of multiple factors including age, class, color, culture, disability, ethnicity, gender, gender identity and expression, immigration status, political ideology, race, religion, sex, and sexual orientation. Social workers appreciate that, as a consequence of difference, a person's life experiences may include oppression, poverty, marginalization, and alienation as well as privilege, power, and acclaim. (p. 5)

Finally, narrative therapies can lead to coping behaviors that can transform the person and his or her environment (Filipp, 1981):

Table 3: National Association of Social Workers
Standards for Cultural Competence in Social Work Practice

❖ Standard 1. Ethics and Values—Social workers shall function in accordance with the values, ethics, and standards of the profession, recognizing how personal and professional values may conflict with or accommodate the needs of diverse clients.

❖ Standard 2. Self-Awareness—Social workers shall seek to develop an understanding of their own personal, cultural values and beliefs as one way of appreciating the importance of multicultural identities in the lives of people.

❖ Standard 3. Cross-Cultural Knowledge—Social workers shall have and continue to develop specialized knowledge and understanding about the history, traditions, values, family systems, and artistic expressions of major client groups that they serve.

❖ Standard 4. Cross-Cultural Skills—Social workers shall use appropriate methodological approaches, skills, and techniques that reflect the workers' understanding of the role of culture in the helping process.

❖ Standard 5. Service Delivery—Social workers shall be knowledgeable about and skillful in the use of services available in the community and broader society and be able to make appropriate referrals for their diverse clients.

❖ Standard 6. Empowerment and Advocacy—Social workers shall be aware of the effect of social policies and programs on diverse client populations, advocating for and with clients whenever appropriate.

❖ Standard 7. Diverse Workforce—Social workers shall support and advocate for recruitment, admissions and hiring, and retention efforts in social work programs and agencies that ensure diversity within the profession.

❖ Standard 8. Professional Education—Social workers shall advocate for and participate in educational and training programs that help advance cultural competence within the profession.

❖ Standard 9. Language Diversity—Social workers shall seek to provide or advocate for the provision of information, referrals, and services in the language appropriate to the client, which may include use of interpreters.

❖ Standard 10. Cross-Cultural Leadership—Social workers shall be able to communicate information about diverse client groups to other professionals.

Source: National Association of Social Workers. (2001). *Standards for cultural competence in social work practice.* Washington, DC: Author.

Assimilation [integration or transcendence] of traumatic experiences is necessary for the creation of a satisfactory life story. Without it, the story will remain incomplete, its central message vulnerable to ambiguity and fragmentation. . . . The most inspiring stories are told by those who manage to transcend early difficulties. It is never too late to restory one's life, starting from the very beginning (Coleman, 1999, p. 136).

End-of-Chapter Questions and Activities

1. Explain the history of the use of the narrative in social science.
2. Distinguish a narrative from a case study that summarizes the main elements of a client's situation.
3. Use the questionnaire developed for this study (see Table 1) and interview an older relative to learn about the discrimination he or she experienced or observed as a child. Learn about the sociohistorical context of the story. How can you use your knowledge to inform practice?

References

Anderson, H., & Goolishian, H. (1992). The client is the expert: A not-knowing approach to therapy. In S. McNamee & K. J. Gergen (Eds.), *Therapy as social construction* (pp. 25–39). Newbury Park, CA: Sage Publications.

Arean, P. A., Perri, M. G., Nezu, A. M., Schein, R., Christopher, F., & Joseph, T. (1993). Comparative effectiveness of social problem-solving therapy and reminiscence therapy as treatments for depression in older adults. *Journal of Counseling and Clinical Psychology, 61,* 1003–1010.

Birren, J. (2001). Foreword. In G. M. Kenyon, P. Clark, & B. de Vries (Eds.), *Narrative gerontology: Theory, research, and practice* (pp. vii–x). New York: Springer.

Bluck, S. (2001). Autobiographical memories: A building block of life narratives. In G. M. Kenyon, P. Clark, & B. de Vries (Eds.), *Narrative gerontology: Theory, research, and practice* (pp. 67–90). New York: Springer.

Butler, R. N. (1968). Toward psychiatry of the life-cycle: Implications of sociopsychologic studies of the aging process for the psychotherapeutic situation. In A. Simon & L. L. Epstein (Eds.), *Aging and modern society* (pp. 233–248). Washington, DC: American Psychiatric Press.

Clark, P. (2001). Narrative gerontology in clinical practice. In G. M. Kenyon, P. Clark, & B. de Vries (Eds.), *Narrative gerontology: Theory, research, and practice* (pp. 193–214). New York: Springer.

Cole, A., & Knowles, J. G. (2001). *Lives in context: The art of life history research.* Walnut Creek, CA: AltaMira.

Coleman, P. G. (1999). Creating a life story: The task of reconciliation. *Gerontologist, 39,* 133–139.

Cooley, C. H. (1964). *Human nature and the social order.* New York: Scribners. (Original work published 1902)

Council on Social Work Education. (2008). *Educational policy and accreditation standards.* Alexandria, VA: Author.

Cross, T. (1998). Understanding family resiliency from a relational world view. In H. I. McCubbin, E. A. Thompson, A. I. Thompson, & J. E. Fromer (Eds.), *Resiliency in Native American and immigrant families* (pp. 143–158). Thousand Oaks, CA: Sage Publications.

Erikson, E. (1963). *Childhood and society* (2nd ed.). New York: W. W. Norton.

Filipp, S.-H. (1981). Ein allgemeines Modell für die Analyse kritischer Lebensereignisse [A general model for the analysis of critical life events]. In S.-H. Filipp (Ed.), *Kritische Lebensereignisse* [Critical life events] (pp. 3–52). Munich: Urban und Schwarzenberg.

Gass, D. (2001). Narrative knowledge and the health care of the elderly. In G. M. Kenyon, P. Clark, & B. de Vries (Eds.), *Narrative gerontology: Theory, research, and practice* (pp. 215–236). New York: Springer.

Gergen, K. J., & Gergen, M. M. (1983). Narrative form and the construction of psychological science. In T. Sarbin (Ed.), *Narrative psychology: The storied nature of human conducts* (pp. 22–44). New York: Praeger.

Greene, R. R. (Ed.). (2002). *Resiliency: An integrated approach to practice, policy, and research.* Washington, DC: NASW Press.

Greene, R. R. (2007). *Social work practice: A risk and resilience perspective.* Monterey, CA: Brooks/Cole.

Gubrium, J. F. (1993). *Speaking of life: Horizons of meaning for nursing home residents.* Hawthorne, NY: Aldine de Gruyter.

Haight, B. K., Michel, Y., & Hendrix, S. (2000). The extended effects of the life review in nursing home residents. *International Journal of Aging and Human Development, 50,* 151–168.

Hallberg, I. R. (2001). A narrative approach to nursing home care of people in difficult situations. In G. M. Kenyon, P. Clark, & B. de Vries (Eds.), *Narrative gerontology: Theory, research, and practice* (pp. 237–272). New York: Springer.

Hunter, K. M., Charon, R., & Coulehan, J. L. (1995). The study of literature in medical education. *Academic Medicine, 70,* 787–794.

Kenyon, G. M., Clark, P., & de Vries, B. (Eds.). (2001). *Narrative gerontology: Theory, research, and practice.* New York: Springer.

Kenyon, G. M., & Randall, W. L. (2001). Narrative gerontology: An overview. In G. M. Kenyon, P. Clark, & B. de Vries (Eds.), *Narrative gerontology: Theory, research, and practice* (pp. 3–8). New York: Springer.

Kirst-Ashman, K. K., & Hull, G. H. (1993). *Understanding generalist practice.* Chicago: Nelson-Hall.

Kropf, N., & Tandy, C. (1998). Narrative therapy with older clients: The use of a meaning making approach. *Clinical Gerontologist, 18*(4), 3–16.

Markus, H. R., & Nurius, P. (1986). Possible selves. *American Psychologist, 41,* 954–969.

McAdams, D. P. (1996). *The stories we live by: Personal myths and making the self.* New York: Guilford Press.

McNamee, S., & Gergen, K. J. (Eds.). (1992). *Therapy as social construction.* Thousand Oaks, CA: Sage Publications.

Mead, G. H. (1934). *Mind, self, and society.* Chicago: University of Chicago Press.

National Association of Social Workers. (2001). *Standards for cultural competence in social work practice.* Washington, DC: Author.

Randall, W. (2001). Storied worlds: Acquiring a narrative perspective on aging, identity, and everyday life. In G. M. Kenyon, P. Clark, & B. de Vries (Eds.), *Narrative gerontology: Theory, research, and practice* (pp. 31–62). New York: Springer.

Ryff, C. D., Marshall, V. W., & Clarke, P. J. (1999). Linking the self and society in social gerontology: Crossing new territory via old questions. In C. D. Ryff & V. W. Marshall (Eds.), *The self and society in aging processes* (pp. 3–41). New York: Springer.

Webster, J. D. (2001). The future of the past: Continuing challenges for reminiscence research. In G. M. Kenyon, P. Clark, & B. de Vries (Eds.), *Narrative gerontology: Theory, research, and practice* (pp. 159–185). New York: Springer.

Webster, J. D., & Haight, B. K. (2002). *Critical advances in reminiscence work: From theory to application.* New York: Springer.

White, M., & Epston, D. (1990). *Narrative means to therapeutic ends.* New York: W. W. Norton.

SOCIAL AND ECONOMIC JUSTICE

This chapter discusses the social and economic justice issues described by the storytellers. (Quotes are taken from the transcripts of all people interviewed for the project as well as those selected for a full chapter presentation. They are identified by a single or double initial.) Various definitions of social and economic justice are provided, and examples are taken from the narratives to illustrate issues of discrimination.

Social and economic markers or indicators may be used to appraise a society's attention to the rights and well-being of its citizenry. These indicators may include educational achievement, the use of technology, infant mortality rates, and poverty, among others. Social and economic injustices can present a risk to development. *Risk* is a factor that influences or increases the (statistical) probability of the onset of stress or negative developmental outcome following adverse events (Masten & Reed, 2002). However, protective factors in the environment, such as a supportive family or teacher, may instill hope and self-confidence that results in a resilient self. As described by N.,

> We had a little house with two rooms, a big room and then a little kitchen. I tell them all the time I remember them cans we put around the house when it rained. They'd play a tune all night long. You'd get in a dry spot, you lay there awhile then and it would move over and drop in your eyes. Then it would start all over again. But we came through it alright. We never really went hungry. I don't know how it would be there, but mother always had some food for us to eat.

This quote illustrates that despite risks, this storyteller remembers how his family coped with its situation, with humor and hope for the future. This ability to overcome adverse events is known as *resilience* and is a major theme of the narratives.

Reflections on Social and Economic Justice

A commitment to social justice begins with self-reflection because it requires an understanding of the contradictions between our values and how we as people act (Freire, 1993). If we understand our own thoughts, we can then make our commitment to equality and a belief in people's capacity to do the same. Self-reflection can help you as a reader answer questions such as the following:

❖ How do you think resources should be allocated in society? What is a valid claim on resources?

❖ What do you as an individual owe society?

❖ What do individuals owe one another?

❖ Do you consider yourself privileged or marginalized? Why?

Social and Economic Well-Being

In 2008, the estimated U.S. per capita personal income was $39,751. According to the *World Bank Atlas*, the gross national income per capita in 2007 ranked the United States 15th among all nations, just behind Sweden and just ahead of the Netherlands. However, the U.S. poverty level of 12.5 percent is not consistent with its high per capita income. A number of countries with similar or lower per capita incomes have lower poverty rates—for example, China at 8 percent and France at 6.2 percent. How do we do on other indicators?

For example, let's look at life expectancy. Note that the life expectancy for American men (74.8 years) and women (80.1 years) is slightly *below* the average for the 30 developed countries. What do you think accounts for this? Is it because the United States does not spend enough on health care? On the contrary, total U.S. spending on health care—which amounts to 15.4 percent of the nation's gross domestic product (GDP)—is far above the 30-country average of 8.9 percent of GDP. How might it be that our Canadian neighbors live, on average, about two years longer yet spend 35 percent less on health care as a percentage of GDP than we do?

U.S. Social Security benefits are not very generous by international standards. U.S. old-age pensions benefits replace about 41.2 percent of earnings compared to 58.6 percent for the 30-country average.

Finally, let's look at the prison population as a possible indicator of political and social well-being. In the United States, 751 per 100,000 people are incarcerated, which is more than five times the 30-country median of 125 people per 100,000. This means that there are approximately 2.3 million people in prison in the United States.

Definitions of Social and Economic Justice

The social work literature refers to a number of definitions of social justice. These are briefly defined here, and you may use them to think about your own beliefs and the stories of the older adults featured here. According to the *Social Work Dictionary*, *social justice* is "an ideal condition in which all members of a society have the same basic rights, protections, opportunities, obligations, and social benefits" (Barker, 2003, pp. 404–405). This definition suggests that historical inequalities should be acknowledged and redressed through specific strategies that "confront discrimination, oppression, and institutional inequities" (Barker, 2003, p. 405). These actions are seen in many of the older adults' narratives.

The promotion of social and economic justice is a core value of the social work profession. The ethical responsibility for social workers to redress inequities is outlined in the National Association of Social Workers (1999) *Code of Ethics*. In addition, according to the Council on Social Work Education (2008) *Educational Policy and Accreditation Standards*, advancing human rights and social and economic justice is one of the core competencies that every social work student must perform.

The Charter of the United Nations promulgated in 1966, recognizes the inherent dignity in, and equal and inalienable rights of, all members of the human family, making social and economic justice a *global consideration* (Council on Social Work Education, 2008). Among the key articles of the Charter are the right to work and to receive fair wages, the right to live without discrimination, equal rights for men and women, freedom from hunger, access to facilities that promote health and education, and the conservation of local cultures. The right to an adequate standard of living encompasses "the right to food, the right to health, the right to water, the right to necessary social services, the right to clothing, and the right to housing" (Center for Economic and Social Rights, n.d.).

Conceptual Differences

The debate about social justice centers on the "tensions between individual liberty and the common good" (Finn & Jacobson, 2008, p. 44). According to Van Soest and Garcia (2003), social workers should understand the conceptions of social justice that underlie society's accountability to the individual, known as *distributive justice*. This involves three major philosophical approaches: (a) utilitarian, (b) libertarian, and (c) egalitarian.

The *utilitarian* approach to social justice explores the distribution of goods, the principles of justice, and the ascriptions of rights that serve the general interest. It examines the relative benefits and harms or costs of a social policy as well as which policy provides the greatest good.

The *libertarian* approach to social justice emphasizes that there is a natural distribution of goods within a given society. Thus, governments should provide citizens with maximum freedom (Nozick, 1974).

The *egalitarian* approach holds that all people are born equal and have the same basic rights to freedom, equal opportunity, access to goods and resources, and self-respect (Rawls, 1971). One of the most widely regarded egalitarian definitions of social justice is that espoused by John Rawls, a political philosopher who proposed that just societies have social contracts that require social, economic, and political institutions to ensure basic rights for all citizens (Galambos, 2008). Rawls (1996) developed a set of principles to govern a *modern social order*, which he defined as "a fair system of cooperation over time, from one generation to the next" (p. 14).

Risk and Power Differentials

Power is another concept related to social and economic risk that should be kept in mind when reading the older adults' narratives presented here. Power exists in all complex societies (Anderson, Carter, & Lowe, 1999) and is related to "one's ability to control or influence, directly or indirectly, the conditions under which one lives" (Goldenberg, 1978, p. 59). Power differentials may occur at the *personal* level, relating to a person's sense of control and affecting one's sense of empowerment; the *interpersonal* level, referring to one's influence over others; the *institutional* level, suggesting the extent to which discrimination is embedded in an organization; or the *structural* level, locating oppression in societal institutions (Cohen, Greene, Lee, Gonzalez, & Evans, 2006).

There is, then, a link between political systems and day-to-day, face-to-face interactions (Giddens, 1984; see Timeline at the end of this chapter for political events). That is, power is inherent in social interaction. According to Foucault (1980), "Power is everywhere . . . because it comes from everywhere" (p. 93). Because power "hovers everywhere and underlies everything," it is a primary concept in the analysis of social life (Giddens, 1984, p. 226). Thus, the narratives of older adults are a means of viewing *microagressions*, the oppressive conditions of everyday life, such as name-calling. As J. recalled when asked about growing up in Central Texas, "Because I was Latin—I mean I wasn't born in Mexico, but they used to tell me at school, 'You Mexican greaser, you'."

Narratives also provide insights into *macroagressions*, or direct larger scale actions that may threaten community survival (Seliger, 1996). As the descendants of Quakertown, a largely middle-class African American community in Denton, Texas, described:

> When the board of trustees of Texas Women's University [TWU] decided they did not want their white daughters walking past the neighborhood where the blacks were living, a petition was submitted to the Denton City Commission to hold a bond election and buy the Quakertown properties to build a park. The bond passed in 1922, and the city began to purchase the homes and land that comprised Quakertown. The Ku Klux Klan came and burned down a house to help make the point clear. The community of Quakertown was destroyed and the property adjacent to TWU is now the home of the city park. [See chapter 5 for a more detailed account.]

Risk as Abuse of Power

Acts of discrimination such as those described in this text may lead to oppression. *Oppression* is a process whereby the dominant group(s) in a society imposes a negative attitude about another group's value or place in the world (Greene, 2008). The oppressor group has more political, economic, and social power (hooks, 1984). It also has control of resources and may have an inordinate influence over cultural life and beliefs. As a result, oppressed groups may be said to be at the *margin*, or outside the main body of power politics (Van Voorhis, 1998).

Through this text, the reader will explore seven common characteristics of inequality in power:

1. inequality in social resources, social position, and political and cultural influences;
2. inequality in opportunities to make use of existing resources;
3. inequality in the division of rights and duties;
4. inequality in implicit or explicit standards of judgment, often leading to differential treatment (in laws, the labor market, educational practices, and so forth);
5. inequality in cultural representations: devaluation of the powerless group, stereotyping, references to the "nature" or (biological) "essence" of the less powerful;
6. inequality in psychological consequences: a "psychology of inferiority" (insecurity, "double-bind" experiences, and sometimes identification with the dominant group) versus a "psychology of superiority" (arrogance, inability to abandon the dominant perspective); and
7. social and cultural tendency to minimize or deny the inequality in power. As a result, potential conflict is often represented as consensus and power inequality as "normal." (Davis, Leijenaar, & Oldersma, 1991, p. 52)

Social Intervention

In a classic book on power relationships written following the Civil Rights movement, Goldenberg (1978) called for social intervention to combat oppression. He suggested that oppression is a condition of being; a stance one is forced to assume that involves a pattern of hopelessness and helplessness. Thus, people who are oppressed may see themselves as being "limited" and "expendable." Goldenberg argued that social interventionists should combat *hostile environments* in which people lack sufficient societal supports by challenging the way society allocates goods and limits power (Chestang, 1972, p. 17; Gitterman & Germain, 2008).

Goldenberg's philosophy is expressed in the Council on Social Work Education (2008) *Educational Policy and Accreditation Standards* as a core competency that social work students are expected to demonstrate. The policy states that

> each person, regardless of position in society, has basic human rights, such as freedom, safety, privacy, an adequate standard of living, health care, and education. Social workers recognize the global interconnections of oppression and are knowledgeable about theories of justice and strategies to promote human and civil rights. Social work incorporates social justice practices in organiza-

tions, institutions, and society to ensure that these basic human rights are
distributed equitably and without prejudice. (p. 5)

Storytelling does not take place in isolation. Rather, stories contain knowledge that is
both personal and political and that offers an understanding of the "social policies, power
relations, and economic realities of the day" (Randall, 2001, p. 39).

For example, R. recalled the many acts of discrimination she faced when growing up:

We had to go shopping in the basement of the stores. We couldn't try
on hats if you wanted to buy a hat. When we went to the grocery stores, you
could be the first person on line. But if a white person came up, they would
wait on them first. Public transportation—here again, I knew when I got on
the bus that I was to go to the back of the bus, even though I was paying the
same fare. In the movie theater, we had to go upstairs. If it was an important
show, the whites occupied the first floor and then the seats on the second
floor. I had to stand to see the movie even if I paid my money.

Risks Faced and Overcome

Although differences exist in how people respond to stress, risk factors have the potential
to affect development adversely. In contrast, *protective factors* are characteristics of a person
and/or environment that are likely to produce a positive developmental outcome. For more
than three decades, risk and resilience research has demonstrated that "at-risk" children and
adolescents can overcome hostile, hazardous environments such as community violence and
civil conflict. In addition, longitudinal studies have revealed that if sufficient protective factors
exist, this positive developmental path can extend into adulthood (Werner & Smith, 1992).

The narratives presented in this book underscore the fact that "patterns of positive adaptation in the context of significant adversity or risk" can continue well into old age (Masten &
Reed, 2002, p. 78). What risks did the storytellers face? How do they describe the challenges
they overcame? The four dimensions of the narrative—personal, interpersonal, sociocultural,
and structural—are used here to give examples of these critical occurrences of discrimination.

Personal Dimensions of Injustice

Personal dimensions of injustice are an individual's expression of how the discrimination felt
to him or her. CS painfully recalled:

I would go out there [Texas Women's University] with my mother to
pick up my dad [who worked there as a baker]. Well I was just a kid, and I
would notice the girls and at that time, they wore uniforms. And I thought
those uniforms were so pretty, and it just made you wish, "Oh, I'll be glad
when I get to [go]," but I wasn't realizing then that I couldn't have gone. If I
had been even at the age to go there, I couldn't have gone.

As a Mexican American child growing up in Central Texas, JD remembered the feeling
of being ignored or on guard. This contributed to a feeling a lack of personal safety:

Sometimes I would be ignored at school, but there were good teachers and I learned a lot. [I felt prejudice] in the stores, theaters, restaurants, and just anywhere you went. The park, a very small park, and we were always on guard because we didn't know when someone was going to do something ugly to us or not.

Interviewer: Tell me more about being on guard.

JD: We would just stay away [from the park] and expect someone to talk ugly to us. We weren't sure of ourselves. Like in the library, the public library, we didn't know if we could check out books or anything.

Interviewer: How did you and your friends overcome this?

JD: We kept quiet. I did. I was always shy, very shy. It [discrimination] made me very shy, like I am inferior. They were intimidating. Because they didn't want Mexicans there. It was a very small community, and they were very prejudiced. It was very hard. They were very mean. Some of them would throw books at me. It was hard because you couldn't talk to the principal or complain, because they wouldn't listen to you. I had more confidence when I settled in to high school. We just tried to survive.

As MH—a Mexican American—pointed out, social injustice can affect personal identity especially during adolescence:

About the Anglos. We used to go to the movies and we had to sit in the balcony not where the Anglos sat. We went to the movies and it said, "For Mexicans only." And yet it made me so mad, I was not a Mexican. I was not born in Mexico. I was born in the United States. We also felt discriminated against in school. I would raise my hand because I knew the answer and they would skip me. They would call on the Anglo girls for the answers.

Interpersonal Dimensions of Injustice

Interpersonal acts of discrimination occur in social interactions. As RC remembered: "I was embarrassed to take tacos for lunch. They would take sandwiches and we would take tacos because we were poor. They would make fun of you, especially the Anglos. There were a lot of people who were mean."

Even in old age, J. recalled the demeaning exchange that took place when he worked for the railroad as a boy:

If you got a drink of water, they had a dipper that was painted black. That was what you drank out of. Bathrooms were usually around the side. So we never questioned all of that. We just went ahead and lived. I remember once. . . .

I think about it a lot. Me and James was I guess around eight years old. We were water boys for the railroad and they had a group of men working on the railroad and we carried water from our well to them, and when they left they owed us some money. They owed us $3 between us. I saw the man a month later. I made a mistake as I went over to him [to ask for the money]. His name was John Smith. I made a mistake by not putting a "Mr." before John. He jumped on to me about it. I was lucky my grandmother came out and got on to him. She said, "You shouldn't talk to a kid like that, talk to me." He just slipped away.

Sociocultural Dimensions of Injustice

The sociocultural dimensions of injustice are embedded in the cultural norms and values of the day. BT remembered the attitude of her generation toward discipline:

They raised us up and taught us discipline. That's something surely even my grandchildren they don't think about now. That's what makes it different in the older generation than they are now. We were respectable. If . . . a neighbor would see them doing something knowing the parents weren't pleased with, they would whoop you, then send you home, and tell your parents and when you got home, you got another one [whooping]. But you can't do that today.

Structural Dimensions of Injustice

The structural dimension of injustice was often enacted in state statutes. For example, there were those that required racially segregated schools. Other "legal" practices, such as that regarding land ownership, might have been "informal," as recalled by RP:

Well, he [a famous football player from their school] went to buy land and they said, they said, "Well, we are thinking about not selling it." They didn't want to sell it to a black. So they later said, "We will sell it to you for more money an acre."

Another structural dimension of social injustice recalled by WH was restrictions on the use of public accommodations such as public swimming pools:

I remember an incident with my younger sister [who wanted to go to the segregated swimming pool]. They have Negro night. You couldn't go in at any time you wanted to. My father would not allow us to go into a segregated pool. I don't know how to swim. . . . I don't know how to skate. And I remember riding by the state fair with my dad and younger sister. She kept asking my father why we couldn't go. "Why can't we go?" A five-year-old did not understand that. And I remember my father wellin' up because he was trying to explain it to her and he really couldn't. And I remember tears coming to his eyes, because he didn't know how to tell his five-year-old, "Because you're black, you're a black girl. It isn't our night to go."

Because the structural dimension of narrative is concerned with the social policies, power relations, and economic conditions of a given society, it provides a means of understanding the diversity and social justice issues of the day. The structural dimensions address the well-being of individuals, families, and groups and whether they are able to obtain basic resources such as housing, food, clothing, and health care. Structural and institutional factors explored in the present text include unemployment, poverty, discrimination, and oppression.

Narrative as Social Reform

Gerontologists argue that storytelling has the power to effect change and may be thought of as a form of social reform in and of itself (Hackman & McDonald, 2002). Storytelling is said to have a ripple effect, influencing the narratives and lives of others (McAdams, 1996). Thus, stories can be rewritten or recast and narratives understood from their local and public dimensions (Gubrium, 2001). Personal stories are anchored in cultural traditions and historical context. For example, in chapter 4, AS tells the story of how he was admitted to the University of Texas at Austin as the first African American social work student. This was a time when the so-called larger story (or "master plot") told by the governor of Texas was that society must retain segregation. When AS was admitted to the School of Social Work, his personal story became political. That is, the actions of the storyteller changed society, making the way for others.

End-of-Chapter Questions and Activities

1. The descendants of Quakertown, five of the storytellers, suggest that although their schools were segregated, they experienced a more positive environment than today's schoolchildren (see chapter 5). Do you agree? Why? See the Harvard Law Center report on schools and desegregation at http://www.civilrightsproject.ucla.edu/aboutus.php
2. Learn more about poverty thresholds in the United States today as compared to 2006 (www.census.gov/hhes/www/poverty/threshld/thresh06.html). Write a one-page paper on who appears most at risk.
3. Select quotes from the chapter that represent statements of marginalization and acclaim/celebration.

References

Anderson, R. E., Carter, L., & Lowe, G. (1999). *Human behavior in the social environment.* Haworth, NY: Aldine de Gruyter.

Barker, R. L. (2003). *The social work dictionary* (5th ed.). Washington, DC: NASW Press.

Center for Economic and Social Rights. (n.d.). *Adequate standard of living.* Retrieved January 4, 2009, from http://cesr.org/adequate?PHPSESSID=32f20b07b76d7a52149ba5397dff4a24

Chestang, L. W. (1972). *Character development in a hostile society* (Occasional Paper No. 3). Chicago: School of Social Service Administration.

Civil rights. (n.d.). Retrieved January 5, 2009, from www.africanamericans.com/civilrights.html

Cohen, H. L., Greene, R. R., Lee, J., Gonzalez, J., & Evans, M. (2006). Older adults who overcame oppression. *Families in Society, 87*(1), 35–42.

Council on Social Work Education. (2008). *Educational policy and accreditation standards.* Alexandria, VA: Author.

Cozzens, L. (1998). *School integration in Little Rock, Arkansas: Introduction.* Retrieved January 5, 2009, from www.watson.org/~lisa/blackhistory/school-integration/lilrock/index.html

Davis, K., Leijenaar, M., & Oldersma, J. (Eds.). (1991). *The gender of power.* Newbury Park, CA: Sage Publications.

Finn, J., & Jacobson, M. (2008). Social justice. In T. Mizrahi & L. E. Davis (Editors-in-Chief), *Encyclopedia of social work* (Vol. 4, pp. 44–52). Washington, DC, and New York: NASW Press and Oxford University Press.

Foucault, M. (1980). *Power/knowledge: Selected interviews and writings.* New York: Pantheon.

Freire, P. (1993). *Pedagogy of the oppressed.* New York: Continuum.

Galambos, C. (2008). A dialogue on social justice. *Journal of Social Work Education, 44,* 1–6.

Giddens, A. (1984). *The constitution of society.* Cambridge, MA: Polity Press.

Gitterman, A., & Germain, C. B. (2008). *The life model of social work practice: Advances in theory and practice* (3rd ed.). New York: Columbia University Press.

Goldenberg, I. I. (1978). *Oppression and social intervention.* Chicago: Nelson-Hall.

Greene, R. R. (Ed.). (2008). *Human behavior theory and social work practice* (3rd ed.). New Brunswick, NJ: Aldine Transaction Press.

Gubrium, J. F. (2001). Narrative, experiences, aging. In G. M. Kenyon, P. Clark, & B. de Vries (Eds.), *Narrative gerontology: Theory, research, and practice* (pp. 19–30). New York: Springer.

Hackman, R. L., & McDonald, S. (2002, May). *Storytelling as a social reform activity for older adults.* Workshop at the Geriatric Mental Health McMaster Summer Institute, Hamilton, Ontario, Canada.

hooks, b. (1984). *Feminist theory: From center to margin.* Boston: South End.

Masten, A. S., & Reed, M. (2002). Resilience in development. In C. R. Snyder & S. J. Lopez (Eds.), *Handbook of positive psychology* (pp. 74–88). New York: Oxford University Press.

McAdams, D. P. (1996). *The stories we live by: Personal myths and making the self.* New York: Guilford Press.

National Association of Social Workers. (1999). *Code of ethics.* Washington, DC: Author.

Nozick, R. (1974). *Anarchy, state, and utopia.* New York: Basic Books.

Randall, W. (2001). Storied worlds: Acquiring a narrative perspective on aging, identity, and everyday life. In G. M. Kenyon, P. Clark, & B. de Vries (Eds.), *Narrative gerontology: Theory, research, and practice* (pp. 31–62). New York: Springer.

Rawls, J. (1971). *A theory of justice.* Cambridge, MA: Harvard University Press.

Rawls, J. (1996). *Political liberalism.* New York: Columbia University Press.

Seliger, M. (1996). *When they came to take my father away.* New York: Arcade.

U.S. Equal Employment Opportunity Commission. (1997). *The ADA: Questions and answers.* Retrieved January 5, 2009, from http://www.eeoc.gov/facts/adaqa2.html

Van Soest, D., & Garcia, B. (2003). *Diversity education for social justice: Mastering teaching skills.* Alexandria, VA: Council on Social Work Education.

Van Voorhis, R. (1998). Culturally relevant practice: Addressing the psychodynamics of oppression. In R. R. Greene & M. Watkins (Eds.), *Serving diverse constituencies: Applying the ecological perspective* (pp. 97–112). New York: Aldine de Gruyter.

Werner, E. E., & Smith, R. (1992). *Overcoming the odds: High-risk children from birth to adulthood.* Ithaca, NY: Cornell University Press.

Timeline: Civil Rights in the United States of America

1619 The first African slaves arrive in Virginia.

1793 A federal fugitive slave law is enacted, providing for the return of slaves who have escaped and crossed state lines.

1808 Congress bans the importation of slaves from Africa.

1863 President Abraham Lincoln issues the Emancipation Proclamation, freeing all slaves "in areas in rebellion."

1865 The 13th Amendment to the U.S. Constitution officially abolishes slavery and involuntary servitude, except as punishment for a crime.

1865 The Ku Klux Klan, a secret militant organization, is founded by veterans of the Confederate Army, the first of many groups to spring up. Its seeks to restore white supremacy in the aftermath of the Civil War through terrorism, violence, and lynching. Its aim is to oppress African Americans, Jews, Catholics, and other minorities.

1868 The 14th Amendment to the U.S. Constitution secures the rights of former slaves and provides a broad definition of citizenship, requiring states to provide equal protection under the law to all persons within their jurisdictions.

1870 The 15th Amendment to the U.S. Constitution prohibits any government in the United States from preventing a citizen from voting based on that citizen's race, color, or previous condition of servitude (i.e., slavery).

1896 In *Plessy v. Ferguson*, the U.S. Supreme Court upholds the concept of "separate-but-equal" public facilities, particularly railway cars.

1909 The first conference of the National Association for the Advancement of Colored People (NAACP) is held in New York City, with 300 black and white Americans in attendance.

1925   Philip Randolph organizes the Brotherhood of Sleeping Car Porters labor union.

1935   Martin Luther King Sr. stages a protest against the segregation of elevators in the Fulton County Courthouse in Atlanta, Georgia.

1941   Philip Randolph issues a call for 100,000 blacks to march on Washington, DC, to protest employment discrimination in the armed services and in industry. Acting to avert this march, President Franklin D. Roosevelt issues Executive Order 8802 forbidding racial discrimination in defense industries and in government service.

1944   The United Negro College Fund is founded.

1950   The Atlanta branch of the NAACP votes to support a lawsuit for equal pay for black teachers.

1953   The Congress on Racial Equality begins sit-ins in Baltimore, Maryland.

1954   In *Brown v. Board of Education of Topeka*, the U.S. Supreme Court declares racial segregation in public schools to be unconstitutional.

1955   A bus boycott is launched in Montgomery, Alabama, after an African American woman, Rosa Parks, refuses to give up her bus seat to a white woman.

1957   Arkansas governor Orval Faubus calls the National Guard to Little Rock Central High School to resist integration and block nine black students from entering the school. President Dwight Eisenhower responds by sending federal troops to protect the students.

1960   The sit-in protest movement begins at a Woolworth's lunch counter in Greensboro, North Carolina. Demonstrators were denied service but allowed to stay seated.

1961   Freedom rides begin in Washington, DC, and demonstrators drive south to challenge segregation.

1963   Police arrest Martin Luther King Jr. and other ministers for demonstrating in Birmingham, Alabama. They then turn fire hoses and dogs on the marchers.

1963   The 24th Amendment to the U.S. Constitution abolishes the poll tax, which had been instituted in 11 Southern states after Reconstruction to make it difficult for blacks to vote.

1964   The Civil Rights Act of 1964 outlaws racial segregation in schools, public places, and employment. It is amended prior to passage to protect women and explicitly include white people for the first time. It forbids racial discrimination in "public accommodations." Public accommodations include hotels, theaters, doctor's offices, pharmacies, retail stores, museums, libraries, parks, private schools, and day care centers.

1965   The National Voting Rights Act of 1965 outlaws discriminatory voting practices responsible for the widespread disenfranchisement of African Americans in the United States.

Sources: *Civil rights* (n.d.); Cozzens (1998); and U.S. Equal Employment Opportunity Commission (1997).

WE HAVE OVERCOME:
RESILIENCE

In the previous chapter, the reader learned how social and economic injustices present potential development risk to individuals, families, and communities. This chapter explores the basic tenets of resilience and how the storytellers overcame adversity, illuminating the characteristics that help individuals, families, and communities cope with and overcome risk.

Risk and resilience theory represents a conceptual shift in human behavior that emphasizes client strengths and inner resources. It offers strategies for mobilizing community strengths, a necessity for 21st-century social work practice (Greene, 2002). The resilience literature offers ways of "thinking about individual and collective assets and situates the focus in a larger social context" (Saleebey, 1997, p. 34).

Lifton (1968) was among the first theorists to describe what he called the *protean* or *resilient self*—a self that can explore numerous directions and opportunities. The resilient self is described as genuine and connected to others and able to respond well to the confusion of historical, economic, and political uncertainties. These narratives illustrate how older adults learned survival skills and ethnic/racial pride, exhibiting characteristics of these adaptive strategies.

Risk and Resilience Theory: Terms

Risk, protective factors, and resilience, the basic terms of resilience theory, are best understood in interaction with one another (see Glossary of Terms at the end of this chapter). *Risk* is "an elevated probability of an undesirable [developmental] outcome" that is precipitated by stressful situations at all ecological systems levels (Masten & Reed, 2002, p. 76). *Protective factors* are characteristics that "predict positive developmental outcomes in the context of risk or adversity" (Masten & Reed, 2002, p. 76). Therefore, protective factors are situations and/or conditions that help individuals to reduce risk and enhance adaptation. They may be internal personal characteristics, such as good problem-solving skills, or external environmental factors, such as viable support networks that modify risks (Rutter, 1987).

For example, at the personal level protective factors encompass variables that contribute to people's innate capacity to interact positively with the environment. These factors are akin to self-efficacy, whereby a person achieves the capacity to control personal events (Bandura, 1977). At the structural or societal level protective factors are related to social, economic, and political resources and the ability to work for the greater good (Lewis & Harrell, 2002).

The term *resilience* refers to self-righting behavior. People who are resilient draw on internal resources, including hope and determination, as well as on external supports such as mutual aid networks (Greene, 2002). Resilience is a "universal capacity which allows a person, group or community to prevent, minimize or overcome the damaging effects of adversity. Resiliency may transform or make stronger the lives of those who are resilient" (Grotberg, 1995, p. 2).

Resilience may not be a single concept. Rather, it may encompass notions of coping, self-efficacy, and competence (Gordon & Song, 1994). Different theorists have somewhat different definitions of resilience. For example, Rutter (1987) defined it as markedly success-ful adaptation following an adverse event; Borden (1992) referred to it as the continuity of personal narrative or life story; whereas Masten (1994) proposed that resilience is a devel-opmental process linked to demonstrated *competence*, or the learned capacity to interact positively with the environment and to complete tasks successfully. Resilience may also be seen as the "development of clusters of self-protective behaviors and strengths" (Greene, 2002, p. 44). Resilience, then, may encompass a wide array of adaptive behaviors.

The philosophy of resilience embodies a strengths-based perspective in which a person's assets and propensities to grow and heal are emphasized. It is also congruent with social work's commitment to the right to self-determination. In a review of definitions in the litera-ture, Stewart, Reid, and Mangham (1997) discovered several common themes:

❖ Resilience consists of a balance between stress and the ability to cope.

❖ Risk factors that stem from multiple stressful life events and protective factors that ameliorate or decrease the negative influence of risk contribute to resilience.

❖ Resilience is dynamic, depending on life context.

❖ Resilience is developmental, because being successful strengthens a person's competence.

❖ Resilience is most important during life transitions.

Resilience has also been defined as a biopsychosocial and spiritual phenomenon involv-ing person–environment exchanges across the life span (Greene, 2002). According to Greene (2002, pp. 41–42), key theoretical assumptions suggest that resilience

❖ occurs across the life course with individuals, families, and communities experiencing unique paths of development;

❖ is linked to life stress and people's unique coping capacity;

❖ involves competence in daily functioning;

❖ may be interactive, having an effect in combination with risk factors;

❖ is enhanced through connection or relatedness with others;

❖ is influenced by diversity, including ethnicity, race, gender, age, sexual orientation, economic status, religious affiliation, and physical and mental ability;

❖ is expressed and affected by multilevel attachments, including family, school, peers, the neighborhood, the community, and society;

❖ is affected by the availability of environmental resources; and

❖ is influenced by power differentials.

Resilience: A Multisystem Phenomenon

Resilience is not restricted to individuals; it also is exhibited in small and large systems. Butler's (1997) definition of resilience captures this notion:

> What we call *resilience* is turning out to be an interactive and systemic phenomenon, the product of a complex relationship of inner strengths and outer help throughout a person's life span. Resilience is not only an individual matter. It is the outward and visible sign of a web of relationships and experiences that teach people mastery, doggedness, love, moral courage, and hope. (p. 26)

A Relational View

An ecological conception of resilience shifts the reader's attention to a systemic, relational perspective. A *relational perspective* to human development is defined as "a process of differentiation and separation in relationships rather than disengagement and separation from relationships" (Genero, 1998, p. 33).

A *systemic perspective* of resilience focuses on the resilience of social systems, that is, resilience as a feature of the collective identity of individuals who are part of systems. A systems model maintains that to understand collective behavior, one must not view each member in isolation. Rather, it is necessary to examine the relationship among members, focusing on the social system's properties in their own right (Greene, 2008).

Resilience can be fostered in all types of systems, including peer groups, schools, the neighborhood, the community, organizations, religious congregations, and societies. The narratives in this text expose the reader to the various influences of these systems on the storytellers.

Resilience and Family Systems

Family resilience is a dynamic quality that varies with family context over time, depending on a family's organizational and communication patterns as well as its belief system (Walsh, 1998). A family resilience approach, according to Walsh (1998), "aims to identify and fortify key interactional processes that enable families to withstand and rebound from disruptive life challenges" (p. 3). Furthermore, family resilience involves "coping and adaptational processes in the family as a unit" (p. 14). Thorton (1998) suggested, "Blacks have forged powerful family ties in the adaptive capacities they have constructed from culture and experience. . . . Foremost in resisting oppression has been the development of a kinship system that has persisted even against great adversity" (pp. 50–51).

PG, for example, remembered how her mother helped her to overcome discrimination during her childhood:

> I think my mother was the strongest person in protecting us from the impact of discrimination. She kept the family very close to her. We were a close-knit family. We weren't exposed a lot to the outside, other than school. We did things as a family, and really the only time we felt poor was when we were in school. Otherwise at home, you know, it was normal. She was a very, very strong person who made us feel loved and stronger and not put down by the discrimination.

EH attributed his ability to overcome oppression to his father:

> I don't know if its conditioning or what. If you think that you can do about anything that you want to do, you pretty much can. . . . I think that everything in my life comes back to my father. He was a person I respected, sometimes I feared. But I always marveled at how he could make—what is the saying—lemonade outta lemons. One of the things he subscribed to was "never let them see you sweat."

Resilience also depends on the fit between family strengths and their specific circumstances. That is,

> family resilience describes the path a family follows as it adapts and prospers in the face of stress, both in the present and over time. Resilient families respond positively to these conditions in unique ways, depending on the context, developmental level, the interactive combination of risk and protective factors, and the family's shared outlook. (Hawley & DeHaan, 1996, p. 293)

Because the relational worldview is a collective, cultural process (Cross, 1998), it can be powerful, particularly in ethnic communities (Daly, Jennings, Beckett, & Leashore, 1995).

Hostile Environments

Ecological theorists suggest that certain niches or social positions occupied by members of the community are devalued and that this process of devaluation by mainstream society can have a negative impact on a child's development. These hostile environments, which lack proper supports and do not allow people to flourish, are said to have a poor goodness of fit between person and environment (Greene, 2008).

Genero (1998) contended that "the study of resiliency in minority families involves coming to grips with the social inequities of racism" (p. 31). Because hostile environments may be detrimental to the development of a positive sense of self (Chestang, 1972), theorists have expressed concern for how best to socialize and foster resilience among children who have an increased risk of experiencing racism and oppression (Billingsley, 1968, 1992; Ogbu, 1985).

The narratives presented in this book support the literature that suggests that resilience is enhanced by an ethnic family's cultural values and provision of mutual psychological support (Genero, 1998; McCubbin, Thompson, Thompson, & Futrell, 1998). Older adults describe their families as helping them cope with a "negative public image" and as teaching survival skills. The storytellers were socialized to have a positive ethnic identity and to develop strategies to resist discrimination (Greene, Taylor, Evans, & Smith, 2002; Miller & MacIntosh, 1999).

JD describes his role as a parent of a Mexican American child:

> We encouraged our children to do the right thing by being interested in what they were doing. Helping them with their homework and being interested in school activities. They all participated in football and things like that. There was a lot of discrimination there. Sometimes they would be discouraged because of things that happened. . . . But I didn't want to discourage them and be against other people. They were brought up in a close community of Mexican Americans and were brought up to be nice and respectful.
>
> We fought for civil rights, all the time and were always concerned for others. It was important to be active in the voting process and to be active in our community.

In sum, a narrative reveals the formation of the self, beginning with the parent–child connection. This continued sense of connection with "other" contributes to the formation of identity and empathy and compassion for others. Most of the narratives in this book concern a time when African Americans and other minority groups experienced social injustice, the denial of legal rights, and social inconsistency (that is, a double standard for blacks and whites) (Chestang, 1972). The family is often described as the "bulwark" against such oppression (see chapter 4). The narratives support the contention made by theorists that parents who proactively socialize their children to withstand discrimination are more likely to raise resilient children (Greene, 2002) (see Table 4).

> ME: As I recall my father's contribution to his family and the African American community in which we lived, I felt a tremendous surge of pride. Notwithstanding his flaws, this pride was not only because of what he gave to me as my father, but also because of what he gave to our community as an African American. He provided our family with a strong, supportive, positive self-image, including an environment of high expectations, and a hard work ethic, which was facilitated by his role modeling.

Table 4: Characteristics of Resilient Children

Psychological/Internal Characteristics

❖ Personal strengths, including a sense of being lovable
❖ Autonomous
❖ Appealing temperament
❖ Achievement oriented
❖ Healthy self-esteem
❖ Trust
❖ Empathy and altruism
❖ Sound locus of control
❖ Intellectual skills

Spiritual Characteristics

❖ Hope
❖ Faith
❖ Belief in God
❖ Morality

Interpersonal/Social Skills

❖ Creativity
❖ Persistence
❖ Humor
❖ Effective communication
❖ Good problem-solving skills
❖ Impulse control
❖ Seeks trusting relationships

Social/External Supports

❖ Structure and rules at home
❖ Parental encouragement of autonomy
❖ Stable home environment
❖ External supports and resources, including trusting relationships
❖ Access to health, education, welfare, and security services
❖ Emotional support outside the family
❖ Stable school environment
❖ Good role models
❖ Affiliated with religious organization

Source: Adapted with permission from International Resilience Project, Civitan International Research Center, University of Alabama, Birmingham.

Resilience and Peer Systems

Peers provide an individual with relationships with people of a similar age and circumstance. The storytellers speak about their sense of belonging and companionship as they engaged in joint activities with peers (Safyer, 1994). As AS put it:

> So there wasn't that much consciousness. When the young white boys that weren't related in some way were in a little fisticuffs with my brother, my cousin, and me, and they say they're gonna tell their parents; we just say we're gonna tell our parents, too. We swim naked in the little gin-tank together and there was just no sense of differences except when school started.

Resilience and School Systems

The narratives reveal that, next to family life, schools played an important function in helping storytellers to recognize inequalities and develop strategies to maintain their sense of competence. Schools acted as agents of adaptation, and teachers could "tip the scale from risk to resilience" by expressing support and respect (Benard, 1997, p. 2). According to S.,

> I do have to say, we had our own black teachers. They took pride in what we learned. The teachers lived in the community. They knew the family background. They sometimes came to the home [if you didn't do your homework].

Resilience and Neighborhood/Community Systems

A community's resilience can depend on whether the community is racially and economically excluded from mainstream society or whether there remains a "collective sense of efficacy" (Sampson, Raudenbush, & Earls, 1997, p. 919). Neighborhoods can be resilient in their own right when they are organized to provide resources, socialize children into the norms for behavior, and provide opportunities for people to participate in the community (Benard, 1991).

Because they acted as part of the support system and buffered the stress of the larger environment, the neighborhoods in which the storytellers grew up were also part of the ecological context of resilience. The narratives reveal that resilience is not only a characteristic of self and family but a feature of community life. Many of the older adults' life stories were set in communities that were faced with legal restrictions based on race and yet remained resilient (see chapter 2). The social fabric of the communities was often strong (Garbarino, 1995), and many exhibited "collective efficacy" (Sampson et al., 1997, p. 919). Home and school often worked together, and teachers acted as role models (see chapter 5).

As ME recalled, some individuals were on the forefront of community activism and "went that extra mile" to be of assistance:

> In the days of strict community segregation, my dad described our town of 10,000 residents as a "one-horse" town, and with amusement and truth called himself 'the horse' in our part of town [the segregated black community]. My stepmother was an elementary schoolteacher and later principal. . . . My father was the person to whom blacks and whites in our community looked for support and resolution when problems occurred. African Americans came to him

for employment recommendations, financial assistance, college recommendations, and advice on how to intervene with the legal system and government.

Resilience and Organizational Systems

Organizations such as the workplace are frequently topics of discussion in this book's narratives. Work is important because it commands a majority of people's waking hours, and income derived from work shapes housing options, educational opportunities, and leisure time activities (Galambos, Livingston, & Greene, 2007).

In addition, as expressed by M., people's personal and professional identities are closely linked with their work:

> I volunteered to go into the military, never with any idea that I would stay beyond the minimal time that I had to stay. After being in the military as an enlisted man for two years, I eventually got commissioned. I guess you can gather that achieving or having some level of status was a very important thing. So being a commissioned officer in the military accorded me that. Being a social worker working in military hospitals, I established friendships with physicians, dentists, and that kind of thing. So it became an attractive sort of option. Then there was a good bit of pride in finally getting commissioned.

Resilience and Religious Systems

The narratives reveal that religious attitudes and religious organizations affected personal and community well-being and resilience. For example, AS recounted:

> Churches—that was the 'hood. That was the main thing. Church was involved in everything. Everybody didn't belong to the same church but they stayed together. Children—the parents made them go to church. You didn't want to, but you would go, and you went with them.

Resilience and Societal Systems

At the societal or macro level, resilience is closely associated with political, legal, and economic issues and policy. It is at this level that social welfare policy comes into play through a "system of interlocking preventative and protective laws and organizations unified by a societal commitment to common goals that are usually associated with a minimum universal access to goods and resources" (Tully, 2002, p. 322). Tully (2002) suggested a five-step model for assessing whether a given policy may enhance or inhibit resiliency:

1. Establish a philosophical statement of the *problem* that needs to be addressed.
2. Determine the feasibility of the political *process* of creating the social policy.
3. Develop the *product*—laws, rules, regulations, and procedures—that can address the problem and be implemented.
4. Put the policy into *practice* and evaluate how well it is working.
5. Understand the evolving nature of *policy* based on societal eras, needs, and beliefs so that continuing action can be taken. (p. 325)

Resilience: Overcoming Critical Events

When reading the narratives of these older adults, the reader will see that the stories consist of a series of critical life events and reveal the meaning the storytellers make of their past and present lives (Bruner, 1999). Critical life events may be self-determined or highly controllable, or they may be beyond a person's control. Discrimination and oppression fall into the category of uncontrollable events and, therefore, may have the power to disrupt or interfere with individual and community development (Baltes, Lindenberger, & Staudinger, 1998). The reader will discover that the narratives tell how this risk was overcome by fostering relatedness, exploring alternative possibilities, creating new meanings, and transcending negative situations (Gergen, 1996). Learning how the storytellers overcame adverse events is key to understanding their resilience.

A person makes meaning of pivotal life events by an appraisal process that may be considered a moment of meaning (Greene, 2007). Paradoxically, the event may be transformational or a marker that gives future direction—a means of envisioning our "future selves" (Markus & Nurius, 1986) as well as envisioning a just society. That critical event presents the individual with an important choice point about what to do next. At the same time, the individual's proactive reaction changes the social order (Diehl, 1999). Thus, the individual's developmental well-being and that of large-scale societal structures are intertwined.

Lewis and Harrell (2002) suggested that as people age, three factors are associated with their resilience: (a) safety and support, (b) affiliation, and (c) altruism. Safety and support are related to resilience because a person's basic needs are ensured. When the basic needs for food, housing, and security are met, the individual feels less risk and may have other aspirations. Affiliation may also strengthen resilience because it is linked to self-satisfaction and health. Altruism can also be linked to resilience because it provides the opportunity for the older adult to live to his or her full potential (see Table 5).

Markers of Resilience

Developmental Milestones

How can the reader know that a person has exhibited resilient behaviors? Markers of resilience are generally considered developmental outcomes, or how a person meets developmental tasks. *Developmental tasks* "are expectations a given society or culture has for behaviors in historical context" in different age periods and situations (Masten & Reed, 2002, p. 76). That is, will a child grow up meeting developmental milestones—or the general norms of the society—to be educated, have a career, marry, or be a "success"?

Personal Qualities

Meeting developmental milestones may be too narrow an interpretation of resilience. Other outcomes involving overcoming adverse events may be better measures. They might include the following:

❖ finding some sense of safety in recognized routines,

Table 5: Resiliency and the Older Adult

Engagement Construct and Practice Level	Resiliency-Based Goal/Need	Resiliency Factor(s)	Worker Guideline
Safety and Support			
Micro	Individual sacred space Personal, immediate physical safety	Psychological well-being; outgoing personality	Guided by client's own story: Perception, cultural framework, memberships included in an ecological framework focused on interacting systems; relationship centered
Meso	Trust of family and peers	Pattern of successful relationships	
Macro	Safe neighborhood and community Access to services such as health care	Economic stability; adequate housing; interested in others and the world	
Affiliation			
Micro	Family (of origin and procreation) creating a sense of belonging	Attitudes toward contribution of aging self	Client as expert
Meso	Small group/social for sense of connection	Attitudes toward contribution of aging elders	Collaboration Consultation—collateral contacts
Macro	Network relationships foster generativity and sense of being needed and helpful	Attitudes toward contribution of aging community	Coalition building
Altruism			
Micro	Reciprocity—spiritual values	Values and beliefs	Concern for community
Meso	Generational benefit—legacy	Common universal values	Family intervention/preservation
Macro	Betterment of the community/environmental factors	Societal/community sanction of values environmental factors	Community development Organizational skills Program development Policy practice

Source: Adapted with permission from Lewis, J., & Harrell, E. (2002). Older adults. In R. R. Greene (Ed.), *Resiliency: An integrated approach to practice, policy, and research* (p. 286). Washington, DC: NASW Press.

❖ obtaining useful information and resources,

❖ resolving stressors,

❖ reestablishing a sense of control or self-mastery or the sense that there are choices to be made, no matter how small,

❖ seeking and providing mutually supportive relationships,

❖ identifying meaning in the event that may be related to spirituality,

❖ maintaining positive emotions and creativity,

❖ gaining an appreciation of newfound strengths, an affirmation of life, or the ability to transcend the event.

Redressing Social Injustice

Perhaps the major marker of resilience mentioned by the older adults in their narratives is striving to redress social and economic injustice. Redressing social and economic injustice requires working to transform or change oppressive and unjust systems into nondiscriminatory and just systems. The narrative content emphasizes how the older adults advocated for social justice, sought legal and societal means to correct abuses, and created a level playing field. As their activism grew, they learned that they had the potential to bring about significant change in people's lives. As J. recounted:

> We were fighting for civil rights, all the time. My husband and my father fought [for] their rights and were always concerned for others. They participated in the voting process, getting people to speak out for themselves and not to let them tear you down. Civil rights was always something we fought for. To be active in the voting process and to be active in our community and what was going on.

End-of-Chapter Questions and Activities

1. Define resilience.
2. Enumerate the sources of successful resilience.
3. Explain the four dimensions of resilience.

References

Baltes, P. B., Lindenberger, U., & Staudinger, U. M. (1998). Life-span theory in developmental psychology. In W. Damon (Series Ed.) & R. M. Lerner (Vol. Ed.), *Handbook of child psychology, Vol. 1: Theoretical models of human development* (5th ed., pp. 1029–1143). New York: John Wiley.

Bandura, A. (1977). *Social learning theory.* Englewood Cliffs, NJ: Prentice Hall.

Benard, B. (1991). *Fostering resilience in kids: Protective factors in the family, school and community.* Portland, OR: Northwest Regional Educational Library.

Benard, B. (1997). *Turning it around for all youth: From risk to resilience* (ERIC Clearinghouse on Urban Education, Institute for Urban and Minority Education, No. 126). Retrieved January 2, 2009, from www.eric.ed.gov/ERICDocs/data/ericdocs2sql/content_storage_01/0000019b/80/14/ff/1b.pdf

Billingsley, A. (1968). *Black families in white America.* Englewood Cliffs, NJ: Prentice Hall.

Billingsley, A. (1992). *Climbing Jacob's ladder.* New York: Simon & Schuster.

Borden, W. (1992). Narrative perspectives in psychosocial intervention following adverse life events. *Social Work, 37,* 125–141.

Bruner, J. (1999). Narratives of aging. *Journal of Aging Studies, 13,* 7–9.

Butler, K. (1997). The anatomy of resilience. *Family Therapy Networker, 3/4,* 22–31.

Chestang, L. W. (1972). *Character development in a hostile society* (Occasional Paper No. 3). Chicago: University of Chicago, School of Social Service Administration.

Cross, T. (1998). Understanding family resiliency from a relational world view. In H. I. McCubbin, E. A. Thompson, A. I. Thompson, & J. E. Fromer (Eds.), *Resiliency in Native American and immigrant families* (pp. 143–158). Thousand Oaks, CA: Sage Publications.

Daly, A., Jennings, J., Beckett, J., & Leashore, B. R. (1995). Effective coping strategies of African Americans. *Social Work, 40,* 240–248.

Diehl, M. (1999). Self-development in adulthood and aging: The role of critical life events. In C. D. Ryff & V. Marshall (Eds.), *The self and society in aging processes* (pp. 150–183). New York: Springer.

Galambos, C., Livingston, N., & Greene, R. (2007). Workplace stressors: A preventive resilience approach. In R. R. Greene (Ed.), *Social work practice: A risk and resilience perspective* (pp. 196–203). Belmont, CA: Brooks/Cole

Garbarino, J. (1995). *Raising children in a socially toxic environment.* San Francisco: Jossey-Bass.

Genero, N. P. (1998). Culture, resiliency, and mutual psychological development. In H. I. McCubbin, E. A. Thompson, A. I. Thompson, & J. A. Futrell (Eds.), *Resiliency in African-American families* (pp. 31–48). Thousand Oaks, CA: Sage Publications.

Gergen, K. J. (1996). Beyond life narratives in the therapeutic encounter. In J. E. Birren, G. M. Kenyon, J.-E. Rush, J. J. F. Schroots, & T. Svensson (Eds.), *Aging and biography: Explorations in adult development* (pp. 205–223). New York: Springer.

Gordon, E. W., & Song, L. D. (1994). Variations in the experience of resilience. In M. C. Wang & E. W. Gordon (Eds.), *Educational resilience in inner-city America* (pp. 27–44). Hillsdale, NJ: Lawrence Erlbaum.

Greene, R. R. (Ed.). (2002). *Resiliency: An integrated approach to practice, policy, and research.* Washington, DC: NASW Press.

Greene, R. R. (2007). *Social work practice: A risk and resilience perspective.* Monterey, CA: Brooks/Cole.

Greene, R. R. (2008). *Human behavior theory and social work practice* (3rd ed.). New Brunswick, NJ: Aldine Transaction Press.

Greene, R. R., Taylor, N. J., Evans, M. L., & Smith, L. A. (2002). Raising children in an oppressive environment. In R. R. Greene (Ed.), *Resiliency: An integrated approach to practice, policy, and research* (pp. 241–276). Washington, DC: NASW Press.

Grotberg, E. H. (1995, September). *The International Resilience Project: Research, application, and policy.* Paper presented at the Symposio International Stress e Violencia, Lisbon, Portugal.

Hawley, D. R., & DeHaan, L. (1996). Toward a definition of family resilience: Integrating life-span and family perspectives. *Family Process, 35,* 283–298.

Lewis, J., & Harrell, E. (2002). Older adults. In R. R. Greene (Ed.), *Resiliency: An integrated approach to practice, policy, and research* (pp. 277–292). Washington, DC: NASW Press.

Lifton, R. J. (1968). Protean man. *Partisan Review, 35,* 13–27.

Markus, H. R., & Nurius, P. (1986). Possible selves. *American Psychologist, 41,* 954–969.

Masten, A. S. (1994). Resilience in individual development: Successful adaptation despite risk and adversity. In M. C. Wang & E. W. Gordon (Eds.), *Educational resilience in inner-city America: Challenges and prospects* (pp. 3–25). Hillsdale, NJ: Lawrence Erlbaum.

Masten, A. S., & Reed, M. (2002). Resilience in development. In C. R. Snyder & S. J. Lopez (Eds.), *Handbook of positive psychology* (pp. 74–88). New York: Oxford University Press.

McCubbin, H. I., Thompson, E. A., Thompson, A. I., & Futrell, J. A. (Eds.). (1998). *Resiliency in African-American families.* Thousand Oaks, CA: Sage Publications.

Miller, D. B., & MacIntosh, R. (1999). Promoting resilience in urban African American adolescents: Racial socialization and identity as protective factors. *Social Work Research, 23,* 159–170.

Ogbu, J. U. (1985). A cultural ecology of competence among inner-city blacks. In M. Spenser, G. K. Brookins & W. R. Allen (Eds.), *The beginnings: The social and affective development of black children* (pp. 45–66). Hilldale, NJ: Lawrence Erlbaum.

Rutter, M. (1987). Psychological resilience and protective mechanisms. *American Journal of Orthopsychiatry, 57,* 316–331.

Safyer, A. W. (1994). The impact of inner-city life on adolescent development: Implications for social work. *Smith College Studies in Social Work, 64,* 153–167.

Saleebey, D. (1997). Is it feasible to teach HBSE from a strengths perspective, in contrast to one emphasizing limitations and weakness? Yes. In M. Bloom & W. C. Klein (Eds.), *Controversial issues in human behavior in the social environment* (pp. 33–48). Boston: Allyn & Bacon.

Sampson, R. J., Raudenbush, S. W., & Earls, F. (1997, August 15). Neighborhoods and violent crime: A multilevel study of collective efficacy. *Science, 277,* 918–924.

Stewart, M., Reid, G., & Mangham, C. (1997). Fostering children's resilience. *Journal of Pediatric Nursing, 12,* 21–31.

Thorton, M. (1998). Indigenous resources and strategic resistance: Informal caregiving and racial socialization. In H. I. McCubbin, E. A. Thompson, A. I. Thompson, & J. A. Futrell (Eds.), *Resiliency in African-American families* (pp. 49–66). Thousand Oaks, CA: Sage Publocations.

Tully, C. (2002). Social work policy. In R. R. Greene (Ed.), *Resiliency: An integrated approach to practice, policy, and research* (pp. 321–336). Washington, DC: NASW Press.

Walsh, F. (1998). *Strengthening family resilience.* New York: Guilford Press.

Glossary of Terms

Bicultural	The ability to integrate two cultural patterns.
Community well-being	Collective positive social justice factors including educational and employment opportunities.
Critical event	A life-shaping occurrence that may include hurricanes, floods, wars, or even genocide.
Culture	A way of life that binds a group together, encompassing values, norms, and beliefs.
Dual perspective	Living in two cultures: the smaller immediate environment and the larger societal system.
Empowerment	A process whereby an individual gains power and increased interpersonal influence.
Ethnicity	People who share cultural patterns over time and develop a sense of peoplehood.
Ethnosystems	A collective of interdependent ethnic groups sharing unique historical and cultural ties bound together by a single political system.
Genogram	A depiction of the extended family across generations.
Hierarchy	The ordering or ranking of people within the system based on power and control.
Hostile environment	A society with social inconsistency and social injustice.
Life review	Looking back and coming to terms with one's life. Sharing memories.
Macroagression	Discrimination experienced as embedded in the larger society.
Macrosystem	A system consisting of the overarching patterns of a given culture including laws, media, and belief systems.
Marginalized group	A group with restricted power in society based on perceived superiority of the group(s) in power.
Microagression	Face-to-face immediate discrimination.
Microsystem	A system comprising a pattern of activities and roles and interpersonal face-to-face relations in the immediate setting.
Minority	People who have limited economic and other power resources.
Mutual aid	People who are supportive to each other and naturally come to the assistance of others.
Narrative	A story or an account of a person's life.
Oppression	Withholding of power by the dominant group(s) in society. The experience of discrimination and limited political power.
Power differentials	Inequality created by how much control and influence, directly or indirectly, people have to shape their own lives.
Powerlessness	A state in which people are hindered from organizing to meet their needs.

Proactive socialization	Socialization that alerts a child to the possibility of discrimination and strategies to take to avert these occurrences.	
Racism	A prejudice that espouses that one group of people is inferior to another and is therefore denied access to resources.	
Race	A social constructed concept of classifying people based on skin color.	
Relational self	A notion of self that is more inclusive of the community and group behavior.	
Resilience	The capacity to overcome adverse events and maintain competence.	
Social system	A structure of interacting and interdependent people.	
	Family	A social system of interdependent persons with its own unique structure, role and communication patterns, and culture.
	Neighborhood	A collective of people who are interdependent and interact.
	Religious	Institutionalized expressions of a faith community.
	School	An educational system created by society to socialize children.
	Societal	The overarching or larger systems of society.
Socialization	The preparation of children to live in a society as competent adults.	
Story dimensions	Individual stories reflect the shared histories and the larger stories of the society. A personal past and a collective history.	
	Personal	My story, beliefs, feelings, meanings, and values.
	Interpersonal	My interactions and mutual influence with others. The significance of others.
	Sociocultural	The social, cultural, and historical context of my story.
	Structural	My involvement with and the affects of larger social systems, such as the laws that affect my access to education and health care.

THE GRADUATE

AS experienced the early childhood tragedy of the death of his father and later the challenges of institutional racism. His ability to overcome adversity is revealed in quotes selected from his narrative.

The quotes introduce the reader to personal, interpersonal, sociocultural, and societal aspects of his resiliency as he surmounted adversity and became an advocate for social and economic justice. Historical events surrounding the time and activities involved in his social activism are discussed.

Biographical Sketch

AS's father died when AS was two years old; he grew up with a single parent and extended family in which his grandparents provided unconditional love. His neighborhood was integrated, but the one-room school he started attending at age four was segregated. When he started the eighth grade, his mother moved the family to Lockhart, Texas, so he could continue with higher levels of schooling. He then discovered that there was a "Mexican school, a white school, and a black school."

AS continued his education despite segregation, and was the first black student and MSW graduate of the University of Texas at Austin School of Social Work. During his career as a social worker, he worked as a counselor at a family service agency, founded a bank, and helped to develop a U.S. Department of Housing and Urban Development-financed housing complex.

AS began his career as a social worker as a caseworker with Houston's Child and Family Center. He later served as a social work education specialist at the U.S. Department of Health and Human Services and as a special assistant to the director of the Department on Manpower and Training Programs in the National Institute of Mental Health. In addition, he was a member of the social work faculties of the University of Houston, Texas Southern University, and the University of the District of Columbia (Kramer, 2005).

Historical Context

AS grew up during a time when African Americans faced many social injustices, including unequal educational opportunities.

Integration of Higher Education

The *Handbook of Texas Online* reports that Texas historically segregated schools on the basis of race and nationality. African and Mexican Americans lived in segregated residential areas and were forced to go to segregated schools, churches, and other places. Most Texas towns and cities had a "Negro quarter" and a "Mexican quarter" (De León & Calvert, 2008).

In 1896, the U.S. Supreme Court in *Plessy v. Ferguson* ruled that the "separate-but-equal" doctrine was constitutional, and this "justified" the segregation of public facilities, including schools and universities, across the country (see chapter 3 for more information). This doctrine went unchallenged for almost 50 years. An early challenge to the separate-but-equal doctrine was *Sweatt v. Painter* in 1950 involving Heman Sweatt, an African American man who applied to the University of Texas School of Law. The law school denied him admission solely on the basis of race. With the help of the National Association for the Advancement of Colored People (NAACP), the Sweatt case advanced to the Supreme Court. In 1950, the Court ruled that a separate school for blacks was not equal to the nationally ranked University of Texas School of Law. Chief Justice Fred M. Vinson wrote the following:

> With such a substantial and significant segment of society excluded, we cannot conclude the education offered [Mr. Sweatt] is substantially equal to that which he would receive if admitted to the University of Texas law school. (cited in Cozzens, 1998)

Although this eventually led to other positive reinterpretations of the 14th Amendment, such as *Brown v. Board of Education of Topeka*, Sweatt faced racial taunts and a visit from the Ku Klux Klan when he arrived on campus. Nevertheless, he persevered and graduated (Cozzens, 1998).

Land Ownership

Although readers are familiar with the oppression of slavery and the lack of voting rights for African Americans, many might not be aware of the discrimination experienced in the pursuit of home- and landownership. As Simpson (1993) argued, historically landownership went hand in hand with the ballot. He argued that the restrictions on landownership undermined emancipation. This was particularly acute in Texas, where mineral rights were sold separately from properties (Robinson, 2005). "To the extent that a landowner also owns the minerals in his tract, he may legally sever such minerals from the surface estates" (Williams & Haigh, 2008).

Four Levels of Resilience in the Life of AS

As indicated, resilience means that people can overcome and even grow through adversity. There often is a critical event, crisis, or difficult life transition that awakens resilience. Resilience refers to self-righting behavior that is set in motion following negative life events such as trauma, stress, or risk. People who are resilient draw on internal resources, including hope and determination, as well as on external support, such as mutual aid networks "to prevent, minimize or overcome the damaging effects of adversity" (Grotberg, 1995, p. 2).

Resilience is a multifaceted concept associated with individual and multisystemic characteristics (Greene, 2002). Cohen, Greene, Lee, Gonzalez, and Evans (2006) adapted the four interrelated dimensions of life stories (Kenyon & Randall, 2001) to categorize resiliency content as (1) the *personal*, involving internal meaning and coherence; (2) the *interpersonal*, including families and friends; (3) the *sociocultural*, referring to social meanings associated with aging and the life course; and (4) the *structural*, encompassing social policies, power relations, and economic conditions. AS's narrative provides examples of each of these levels and the interrelationships among them.

Personal

Resilience is the ability "to function psychologically at a level far greater than expected given a person's earlier developmental experiences" (Higgins, 1994, p. 17). As can be seen in AS's life story, he had a sense of self-esteem that came from support that helped him deal with the trauma of the death of his father:

> I had personally sensed that [family love] has been a bulwark against the challenges I have faced in dealing with racism, with oppression, with rejection. Because my response inwardly, before I was able to verbalize it, if you could really know how beautiful I am, how important I am, how special, instead of running away from me, you'd be running toward me.

AS also recalled the following:

> Love alone is not enough. You got to know something. And have some conviction of the efficacy of that knowing. But getting back to the concept of resiliency. Faith growing out of the conviction of one's somebodiness, one's sense of belonging, one's sense of caring. And I think in a way that one can't really give it if one didn't get it. No matter how, in what amount, there has to be something that one receives in order that one can give.

> *Interviewer:* Does that drive your social work as well? Your practice and leadership in that area?

> *AS:* Oh, yes. I said earlier that caring is basic, but knowing, interwoven with that caring, the sky's the limit. It's . . . it's that which helps one to be capable of maintaining hope. And I forget the author of the statement, but as I recall, "Hope is, hope is certainty." I'll have to come back to that.

AS provided another description of his childhood racial awakening:

> There was just no sense of differences except when school started. Our school was just this little unpainted building, I would say it must have been about maybe 1,200 square feet, because the 18 to 20 children from primer

through seventh grade were all in the same room but sectioned off according to grade level. It was not really until I was transferred for my eighth grade that I really began to discover the differences. Because the bus that carried my peers to school couldn't or wouldn't carry me to school. So my cousin, my brother, and I rode a milk truck. And when the milk truck couldn't negotiate those boggy roads in the winter, that time of the year, we couldn't get to school, because it was nine miles away.

Interpersonal

AS attributed the "unequivocal" love of his extended family to his ability to face and overcome the life challenges of discrimination and oppression he later faced. He described this personal feeling as "a bulwark against the [later] challenges I have faced in dealing with racism."

AS began his narrative, talking to the interviewer about his earliest memories of adversity.

Interviewer: Sharing one's life story really is a gift to the community and to the school of social work. Let me just tell you about this project. It's been a two-year journey learning about resilience from people who have overcome adverse events. It may have been the Nazi Holocaust, it may have been a difficulty in their personal life, and it may have been discrimination or oppression. I learn from each person about their strengths, and influence on their family and their community. We learn what they have done to be successful despite adversities. We want to know what's inherent in human beings that make them successful despite these events.

AS: Well I can say that having lived 77 years I have a few comments to make about resiliency and coping, the mechanism of coping. It's kind of difficult how to begin. You mentioned earlier, the five-year period, a critical point of reference in terms in recalling certain events. I'm thinking back now to my beginnings around 4. I want to say first of all that there was a tragedy in my parent's life, the death of my father when I was two in a railroad accident. I have a sibling who is 16 months my junior, but he was just an infant, so my mother returned home to her parents to live, upon my father's death. So, in a way I'm from the proverbial one-parent extended family.

AS shares many of the characteristics associated with children who are resilient, including trusting relationships and a stable home environment (see Table 4 in chapter 3). AS speaks of the bonding and acceptance expressed in his family that "just shone out," and made him secure in his environment.

A family's adaptation to stress may be the most critical interpersonal experience affecting resilience (Hawley & DeHaan, 1996, p. 284). Many researchers believe that resilient children grow up in warm, affectionate home environments (Garmezy, 1993; Werner, 1993).

AS expressed this well:

> Back to the forces that enabled me to cope in a fashion: I was the first grand-child on either side of the family to be born, a very special place. My father's name was August, my name was August, and I'm a junior. If I had any reason to feel guilt, it was because of that special place. Unequivocal love, some rivalry between grandparents as to where it was that I would be. But my grandmother on my maternal side was so very strong a force, so there was no such thing as her babies going anywhere else. But that sense of belongingness, that somebodiness, that sense of being special among people of color, black people in particular.

AS's early childhood was spent with white and black friends who bonded and accepted one another. This interpersonal experience in a secure environment also contributed to his resilience.

Sociocultural

The sociocultural dimensions of resilience are apparent in the social meanings and context of the day. These social meanings shape workplace relationships and may include cultural, ethnic, and gender stories (Kenyon & Randall, 2001). Stories about the Jim Crow period of history have been subjugated, and as a result the history of African Americans and other minorities can be obscured (Saleebey, 1997).

AS described his childhood neighborhood as integrated. He described his interracial lineage and its role in history.

> My community was evenly divided between so-called white people and Negroes. Maybe there were 300 total in this population, but my grandparents, both maternal and paternal, lived the equivalent of four blocks from one another. . . . So in this community in Dale, Texas, I guess my closest neighbor was a block away, the M. family. The M.s and the S.s were like family, except they were white. But it was a community that antedated the integration movement because there was some inter-racial marriage. As a matter of fact, my grandfather's father was Anglo, and so was my grandmother's mother.
>
> We had relatives that established the Chisholm

The Chisholm Trail

The Chisholm Trail was the major route for livestock traveling out of Texas to the Kansas railroads, where they were sold and shipped eastward. Although the trail was only used from 1867 to 1884, cattle driving provided a steady income and made the cowboy a folk hero. Trail teams consisted of a trail boss, 10 cowboys, a cook, and a horse wrangler. As many as 2,500 cattle would graze along the trail (Worcester, 2008).

Trail for Caldwell County and this part of the state. And the same relative rode with [Lyndon B. Johnson's] grandfather from Texas to the western part of the state to Kansas on the cattle drive.

Structural

The structural dimensions of resilience include both the ecological context of neighborhoods and the overarching social, political, legal, economic, and value patterns of the larger society (Greene, 2002). These social constructs enable one to examine resilience as a large-scale phenomenon. Structural dimensions of resilience also relate to the institutional structures/ organizations, such as schools, that carry out community functions. In the case of AS, the schools were segregated, were inadequately financed, and had poor facilities (De León & Calvert, 2008); yet he fondly remembered going to the one-room schoolhouse:

> My aunt discovered I was at the school grounds [when I was four]. It was across the road from my house—this one-room schoolhouse where she was a teacher. So she petitioned my mother and my grandmother to allow me to enroll in the school formally because I was at the school grounds all the time anyway. So, at age four, I begin my formal education process, the pre-primer. So I virtually grew up on the school grounds, which put me ahead of my peers, in terms of grade level. Additionally, my peers were pretty much always older than me. I spent this time in a one-room school that had all the seven grades from the primer to the seventh grade.

When AS started the eighth grade, his mother moved the family to a larger town so he could continue with higher levels of schooling. AS was very aware of institutional racism. When AS applied for admission to the University of Texas at Austin School of Social Work, then-Governor Beauford H. Jester was still trying to preserve a segregated "separate-but-equal" system of education. Nevertheless, AS was admitted to the School of Social Work, class of 1953, and was the first African American to receive a master's degree in social work there. As AS stated:

> When I was interviewed for the School of Social Work by the regional director, the Governor of Texas at the time, the late Governor Jester, said Negroes would go to the university over his dead body. The admissions director interviewed me and I was admitted that week.

Interviewer: When was that?

AS: In 1951, in August of 1951. I was not prepared to go to the School of Social Work. I majored in sociology and minored in education, with a certification to teach at the high school level. So I was going to teach, because that was what I thought I could do, that's what I was prepared to do. But I learned that the School of Social Work had opened the year before and that I might have a shake as a sociology

major. When Mrs. Peterson interviewed me, in spite of those
inflammatory remarks made by the governor, I was in fact
admitted, and did in fact graduate, of course. But ironically
when our son graduated from high school, from Strake Jesuit
High School, and moved to [the University of Texas], he
and his buddy from Strake moved into Jester, the dormitory
named after the governor who made those remarks.

A neighborhood or community can be resilient, and this can affect individual development and well-being. This is demonstrated in AS's reflections about his lineage and the importance of home/property ownership. AS's resilience was fostered not only by the support of his extended family but by their economic stability and relative well-being:

My dad's parents were shopkeepers and farmers. As a matter of fact, my
mother and my father were living in the farm place of my father's parents, but
they moved to this community Dale and opened up their own store. He was
sort of an entrepreneur. He had a molasses meal mill where people brought
their cane and had it ground into syrup, and as he was just an entrepreneur,
my grandfather on my mother's side was a railroad section hand, and in fact
that's where my father was killed on the railroad.

Home ownership was another important structural aspect that contributed to AS's sense of security and resiliency.

AS: No question about it [home ownership]. Most of my peers,
who were not related by blood, were like sharecroppers, they
were renters, and they did not own property. As far back as
I can remember, and as many of my paternal and maternal
grandparents were concerned, they were all property owners.

Interviewer: How does that affect your sense of security?

AS: There's no question. Because it's been instilled in us, as out-
growths of the environment, that if you're a renter, not a
property owner, you are in fact a slave because you can be told
when to move, how much you got to pay if you don't move.
We never had to experience that. It might have been different if
circumstances were different. In fact, if my father had not been
killed, my mother had not secured insurance, that meant she
paid for my grandfather's on her side's properties. They were
part owners but it was mortgaged property. Not the house
in which they lived, but the farm 2½ miles northeast of Dale,
Texas. So that sense of nobody can move us, nobody can tell us
when to go, where to go, how to go. . . .

Activism

The family is the first "narrative environment" in which children learn what they can and cannot be and in what ways they will "story their lives" (Randall, 2001, p. 42). AS proudly recalled his daughter's activism:

> Our daughter was in college, she with her peers. [She was in a demonstration] to keep the campus from encapsulating the surrounding areas where they were going to bulldoze these trees down, these magnificent trees. She and her peers allowed themselves to be chained to the trees so they wouldn't be bulldozed away.

AS's life also demonstrates the power of recovery and the maintenance of competence following early adverse events. As did many of the storytellers, he went on to engage in community activism. Realizing that many African American communities did not have banks, AS and a group of community-service-minded people founded the Riverside Bank, now known as Unity National Bank. It is located in the heart of Houston's Third Ward, a low-income community, and is the only African American owned bank in Texas (A Unity Community, n.d.).

AS suggested that such activism centers on people's hope for the future.

Interviewer: Well, what would you say to young people today about hope? Can they latch onto something if they do what?

AS: Well, let me give you an example. It's just a minor thing. On reflection, I had a friend who was a Pullman car porter, and during the time that he was traveling cross-country with these bankers,

Banking and Lending

Historically, women and racial minorities have been denied access to capital from formal financial institutions, leaving them unable to borrow, save, or invest.

Community Investing Institutions (CIIs) are established to serve populations disenfranchised from traditional banking institutions. They enable women and minorities to purchase cars, buy homes, and receive loans to pay off debts. Participants in CII are not only borrowers but also leaders and lenders in their communities. One example of a CII is Unity National Bank, the only CII and only African American–owned bank in Texas. Unity National Bank was chartered in 1985 and is insured by the Federal Deposit Insurance Corporation. Its mission is to "support the underserved communities that have historically sort of been under-banked and underserved" (Community Investing Center, 2005). The Bank has worked extensively with potential homeowners and small businesses and may even occasionally make short-term paycheck loans for groceries (Community Investing Center, 2005).

and investment bankers or whatever, he was admonished to study to learn how to become a broker, selling stocks, bonds. So he got me sorta interested in investment, but he said one day, "We're gonna have a bank." I said, "I don't know anything about banking and finance from the standpoint of a business administration degree and the knowledge base. But I know that there is a need because there are people in this city who can't borrow money for profit purposes. They can buy a car, but they won't establish business. . . . I know something about groups and keeping them on task, and establishing goals, that sort of thing. So let's identify some people and let's see what happens."

Well, on the strength of that, Unity National Bank in Houston, Texas—which used to be Riverside when it was established in the mid-1960s—was based on a little know-how, and a lot of faith. Because I said to him, in social work I learned that social workers are masters of resource identification, maintenance, and utilization and people resources. So we put together a group of six or seven people. And the result is that that bank is a living testimony to institution building.

Now, socially having learned through my work with the family agency that there were a lot of families who were exploited by unscrupulous absentee landlords because they couldn't buy houses, and where they could buy them they were "redlined" so they couldn't get [a loan]. . . . So, we organized a group of church trustees from Wesley Church in Houston. I was a member of that church at the time, so we built a 252-unit federally subsidized housing unit, $3.5 million dollar project. We didn't say that white people couldn't be housed there, nor Hispanics. It was people in need of housing, and you can qualify based on [an income] scale. . . . We had a 68-capacity year-round Head Start facility built in. The manager at the time, who was also a trustee, was insistent that a retired schoolteacher take over the administration of that facility. Trustees voted five times over as many months to give that to the so-called poverty program, the West Coast Community Services Organization. In exchange, . . . they would provide the teacher ratio, teacher's assistance, the epitome of year-round Head Start, dental

care, medical care, the equivalent of $200,000 a year in ser-
vices to the families of those 68 youth. And we didn't need
the income from that unit, but we did it. Now 40 years later,
that 252-unit housing program has survived.

Suggested End-of-Chapter Study Questions

1. List examples (using quotes or behaviors) of the four levels of narrative that you read in
   the life story of AS:
   a. Structural (including policy and legislation)
   b. Sociocultural
   c. Interpersonal
   d. Personal
2. How does AS explain his resilience?
3. How does AS explain how "difference" has shaped his life?

References

A unity community. (n.d.). Retrieved January 8, 2009, from http://www.aframnews.com/html/2004-04-01/lead3.htm

Cohen, H. L., Greene, R. R., Lee, J., Gonzalez, J., & Evans, M. (2006). Older adults who overcame oppression. *Families in Society, 87* (1), 35–42.

Community Investing Center. (2005). *Women & minorities.* Retrieved April 24, 2007, from http://www.communityinvest.org/impact/minorities.cfm

Cozzens, L. (1998). *School integration in universities.* Retrieved January 2, 2009, from http://www.watson.org/~lisa/blackhistory/early-civilrights/higher.html

De León, A., & Calvert, R. (2008). *Segregation.* Retrieved January 2, 2009, from http://www.tshaonline.org/handbook/online/articles/SS/pks1.html

Garmezy, N. (1993). Children in poverty: Resilience despite risk. *Psychiatry, 56,* 127–136.

Greene, R. R. (Ed.). (2002). *Resiliency: An integrated approach to practice, policy, and research.* Washington, DC: NASW Press.

Grotberg, E. H. (1995, September). *The International Resilience Project: Research, application, and policy.* Paper presented at the Symposio International Stress e Violencia, Lisbon, Portugal.

Hawley, D. R., & DeHaan, L. (1996). Toward a definition of family resilience: Integrating life-span and family perspectives. *Family Process, 35,* 283–298.

Higgins, G. (1994). *Resilient adults: Overcoming a cruel past.* San Francisco: Josey Bass.

Kenyon, G. M., & Randall, W. L. (2001). Narrative gerontology: An overview. In G. M. Kenyon, P. Clark, & B. de Vries (Eds.), *Narrative gerontology: Theory, research, and practice* (pp. 3–8). New York: Springer.

Kramer, K. (2005). After retirement, ITSSW alums. *Utopia, 7*(1), 15.

Randall, W. (2001). Storied worlds: Acquiring a narrative perspective on aging, identity, and everyday life. In G. M. Kenyon, P. Clark, & B. de Vries (Eds.), *Narrative gerontology: Theory, research, and practice* (pp. 31–62). New York: Springer.

Robinson, L. (2005, April). *Oil play: Surface versus mineral: Mineral owners call the shots.* Retrieved January 8, 2009, from http://www.tlma.org/oilplay.htm

Saleebey, D. (1997). Is it feasible to teach HBSE from a strengths perspective, in contrast to one emphasizing limitations and weakness? Yes. In M. Bloom & W. C. Klein (Eds.), *Controversial issues in human behavior in the social environment* (pp. 33–48). Boston: Allyn & Bacon.

Simpson, B. (1993). Land & the ballot: Securing the fruits of emancipation. *Pennsylvania History, 60,* 176–192.

Werner, E. (1993). Risk, resilience, and recovery: Perspectives from the Kauai longitudinal study. *Development and Psychopathology, 5,* 503–515.

Williams, H. R., & Haigh, B. R. (2008). *Mineral rights and royalties.* Retrieved January 8, 2009, from http://www.tshaonline.org/handbook/online/articles/MM/gym1_print.html

Worcester, D. E. (2008). *Chisholm Trail.* Available at http://www.tshaonline.org/handbook/online/articles/CC/ayc2.html

MEMORIES OF QUAKERTOWN

Biographical Sketch

From the mid-1870s through the early 1920s, Quakertown was a middle-class, African American neighborhood of Denton, Texas. During the 1880s, the Quakertown residents built schools, churches, businesses, and civic organizations to support the growing number of black families living there. By the 1910s, Quakertown was a thriving community of more than 50 middle- and working-class families (see http://dentoncounty.com). Many families had arrived in groups following Reconstruction, escaping from areas where former slave owners tried to pressure them to return to plantations.

The demise of Quakertown began in 1920, when the trustees of the College of Industrial Arts (now Texas Women's University) decided that they did not want their white daughters walking through the black Quakertown neighborhood. A petition was submitted to the Denton City Commission to hold a bond election to buy the Quakertown properties and build a city park. The bond issue passed in 1922, and the city began to purchase the homes and land that composed Quakertown.

The residents either sold their homes or had their homes moved to the other side of the railroad tracks. The community of Quakertown was thus destroyed, and what was a thriving black community became a city park.

Historical Times

Many of the Quakertown residents had moved there during Reconstruction, from the end of the Civil War to 1877. Reconstruction initiatives addressed how to transition newly freed slaves and how to restore self-government to secessionist southern states. During this period,

Timeline of Federal Civil Rights Laws

1866: Congress passes a law declaring all persons born in the United States to be citizens, regardless of race or color, guaranteeing the rights to make contracts, sue, bear witness in court, and own private property.

1871: Congress passes a law providing for a cause of action in federal court for the interference with a federal civil right by a person acting under the authority of state law.

1875: Congress passes a law prohibiting discrimination in public accommodations based on race. This law is overturned by the U.S. Supreme Court in 1883 as an unconstitutional exercise of congressional authority.

1945: Congress considers a civil rights bill for the first time in 70 years, but the legislation does not advance. A civil rights bill will be introduced every year until 1957, but none will make it to a floor vote in either chamber.

1957: Congress passes the Civil Rights Act of 1957, the first federal civil rights bill adopted since 1875. This legislation was crafted by the Eisenhower Justice Department to set up the federal government as protector of voting rights for African Americans. The bill creates the U.S. Commission on Civil Rights, the Civil Rights Division of the U.S. Department of Justice, and institutes a cause of action in federal court for the denial of voting rights. The bill almost fails in the Senate when Senator Strom Thurmond (R-SC) filibusters the legislation by speaking for more than 24 consecutive hours on the Senate floor. In the end, it takes a substantial compromise—striking the ability of the Attorney General to intervene in state civil rights cases and providing a trial by (in practice, all-white) jury in federal voting rights cases—to get the measure through Congress. This compromise substantially divides the civil rights community.

1960: Congress passes the Civil Rights Act of 1960. This legislation expands the 1957 law by requiring election authorities to make registration records available for inspection by the Justice Department and by enabling federal judges to appoint referees to hear claims that state election officials denied individuals the right to register and vote based on race. Again, southern senators attempt to block its passage, with a group staging the longest filibuster—more than 43 consecutive hours—in Senate history. A cloture vote ends disastrously, not even garnering a majority, and in the end the bill passes the Senate only when its proponents agree to remove a more substantial role for the Attorney General from the proposed law.

1963: Congress passes the Equal Pay Act of 1963. This legislation prohibits wage differentials based on sex. As a part of the Fair Labor Standards Act, however, the provision requiring wage equity does not apply to executive, administrative, or professional employees.

1964: Congress passes the landmark Civil Rights Act of 1964. This legislation is, at last, a robust civil rights law that bars discrimination based on race, color, religion, sex, or national origin in employment, in public accommodations, and by recipients of federal funds. The bill makes it out of the House Judiciary Committee only under the threat of a discharge petition and has to again overcome a filibuster by southern senators. The addition of "sex" as a protected category is, arguably, an attempt by a Texas representative to sabotage the bill. At the time of the adoption of this bill, 28 states had already enacted fair employment laws that prohibited discrimination on the basis of race.

1965: Congress passes the Voting Rights Act of 1965. This legislation thoroughly addresses the denial of voting rights based on race by outlawing literacy tests for voters, providing federal voter registration in areas of low minority registration, and providing Justice Department oversight of and approval for changes to voting laws in areas with low minority registration. Again, the bill has to overcome a concerted effort to filibuster by southern senators.

1967: Congress passes the Age Discrimination in Employment Act. This legislation outlaws employment discrimination based on age (of persons 40 years of age or older).

1968: Congress passes the Civil Rights Act of 1968 (also known as the Fair Housing Act). This legislation outlaws discrimination in housing based on race, color, religion, sex, or national origin.

1968: Congress passes the Architectural Barriers Act. This legislation requires that facilities designed, built, altered, or leased with federal funds be accessible to persons with disabilities.

1972: Congress passes Title IX of the Education Amendments of 1972. This legislation outlaws discrimination based on gender in education programs and activities that receive federal funding. Another provision of the Education Amendments removes the "blue-collar jobs" limitation on the Equal Pay Act of 1963.

1973: Congress passes the Rehabilitation Act of 1973. This legislation prohibits discrimination based on disability in any program or activity receiving federal funding.

1974: Congress passes the Equal Educational Opportunities Act. This legislation prohibits segregating students on the basis of race, color, or national origin as well as discriminating against faculty and staff on those bases. This bill also requires school districts to take action to overcome students' language barriers that impede equal participation in educational programs.

1975: Congress passes the Pregnancy Discrimination Act. In response to narrowing judicial interpretations of Title VII's prohibition on sex discrimination, this legislation is adopted to bar employment discrimination based on pregnancy, childbirth, or related medical conditions.

1975: Congress passes the Age Discrimination Act of 1975. This legislation prohibits discrimination on the basis of age in any program or activity receiving federal funding.

1990: Congress passes the Americans with Disabilities Act. This legislation bolsters the Rehabilitation Act by prohibiting discrimination based on disability in employment and public accommodations. Congress affirmatively excludes transsexuals and current substance abusers from the bill's protections.

Sources: http://www.hrcbackstory.org/2007/11/timeline-of-fed.html; and Public Broadcasting Service (n.d.).

the 13th, 14th, and 15th Amendments to the U.S. Constitution were enacted, spelling out the role of the federal government in protecting citizens' rights.

However, many of the gains blacks made during Reconstruction were wiped out with the backlash against integration and the passage of Jim Crow laws. These laws institutionalized discrimination and segregation against black people mostly practiced in the American South from the end of Reconstruction until the passage of civil rights legislation in the mid-20th century. For example, the state of Texas enacted 27 Jim Crow laws limiting access to education, voting rights, marriage, and the use of public accommodations. By legalizing segregation and the disenfranchisement of African Americans, every state in the former Confederacy had put into place a system of white supremacy by 1910 (Davis, n.d.).

The descendents of Quakertown recalled sundown laws, according to which nonwhites, especially African Americans, were not permitted in certain neighborhoods after the sun went down. People of color found in these designated areas would be subject to harassment, threats, and even lynching.

> *Descendent A:* And he [my older brother] often shared many experiences [about life at that time]. At night, you know, there were certain areas that the blacks could not be caught in, especially around [Texas Women's University] and North Texas University and the areas there. You had to be off the square before dark because there would be groups of young white guys that would chase them off. We had to be off the square at that time or nightfall.

Personal Aspects of Resilience

The descendents of Quakertown remembered not being able to go to town and sit at the neighborhood soda fountain. They would have to enter and leave by a back door.

> *Descendent B:* I guess that was one of the things I noticed growing up. Then when we went to the square of town, other kids could go in and sit at the ice cream counter where the soda fountains were, they could go and sit and drink and eat there. But if we bought something, we had to get it and take it in our hands and go on out with it to eat it. We couldn't sit on the stoop. I guess all those little things as a child, I noticed all those differences.

Descendents recounted Texas Jim Crow laws that segregated public accommodations. They were particularly vocal about laws that restricted seating at movie theaters.

> *Descendent D:* [At] the movies, we had to go up in the balcony. At the time the western movies were the big thing the kids went to see on weekends, but we had to crowd in the balcony. We

couldn't sit, we couldn't even enter in the front, and we had
to go to the back to enter the theater. All those things, I was
a kid but I noticed all those differences. Those were some of
the things that stood out for me as a child growing up.

According to the Center for Economic and Social Rights, the right to education requires free and compulsory primary level education as well as equal access to every level of education (see http://cesr.org/education). Adequate facilities and buildings should also be available. The descendents of Quakertown were aggrieved about the inequality of "white" and "black" schools.

Descendent C: I guess I noticed the difference when I was real young
because as I said, I was in elementary school and we would
go to give programs at the schools and the teachers would
take us out there to do the programs for the kids out there
[in other schools], so I really noticed the difference in the
buildings—the comfort.

One descendent reflected on the ways in which her self-image and accomplishments were affected by the discrimination she experienced as a young child. Her comments were reminiscent of the work of Robert Coles (1967, 1986a, 1986b), a child psychiatrist who used the narrative form to interview children and structure his work during the desegregation of New Orleans schools in the early 1960s. Similar to the storytellers here, Coles's narratives revealed that children have a compelling sense of right and wrong.

Descendent E: In other words, we were just kind of second class I guess is
what they would call us. . . . As she said, we had no books,
some of them they were torn up, had been written all in.
The kids tried to have a football team and a basketball team,
their uniforms came from the white school all raggedy, but
we had a number one football team and we had no gym.
They stored things under the school. That's where they
kept their football clothes and things, under the school, and
that's what they called the dugout.

Descendent B: When I came along in the school, they had a little room in
the back where they put all the junk they would bring from
the white school for the football players. They had to go into
this little room where they kept the books—the library they
called it. All this equipment, just as musty, all sweaty, but
that was the only way they could get these uniforms to play.

Descendent A: Yes, but we had a number one football team. We had a
number one coach, Mr. Miller. He was tough on them boys.
He was the first one to integrate North Texas.

Segregated Schools: Separate and Unequal

In the half century that passed between the time the Supreme Court gave legitimacy to the concept "separate but equal" in 1896 and the recognition in *Brown v. Board of Education of Topeka* in 1954 that "separate" was not, and in fact could not be, "equal," lower courts routinely found against black plaintiffs despite overwhelming evidence that the schools of the plaintiffs' children were underfunded, rundown, and dilapidated.

The *Brown* case consolidated the appeals to the Supreme Court of five separate cases, all of which were based on evidence of blatantly unequal schooling for black and white students. In each case, lower courts had ruled against the plaintiffs, upholding the separate-but-equal doctrine.

Clarendon County, South Carolina, was one of the five plaintiffs in the *Brown* case. The county spent four times as much on white schools as on black schools. As a result of underfunding, black schools in the county were dilapidated and overcrowded. White students had new textbooks while black students had used ones; the highest paid black teacher earned less than the lowest paid white teacher. Further, white students rode buses to school, whereas black students had to walk.

Conditions in Moton High School in Farmville, Virginia, another plaintiff in the *Brown* case, were badly affected by underfunding: The school did not have a gymnasium, a cafeteria, or teachers' restrooms; teachers and students had neither desks nor blackboards; and classrooms were overcrowded. To handle the extra students, some classes were held in temporary tar paper shacks; it was so cold in winter that students and teachers had to keep their coats on. Despite these deplorable conditions, the school's requests for additional funding were rejected by the all-white school board.

Despite the existence of a well-maintained, spacious high school in Claymont, Delaware, segregation forced parents to send their children on a public bus to attend the rundown Howard High School in downtown Wilmington. The school was Delaware's sole business and college-preparatory school for African American students. Parents expressed concerns about class size, teacher qualifications, and curriculum. Moreover, Howard students interested in vocational training were required to walk several blocks to a nearby annex to attend classes offered only after the conclusion of the normal school day. Thus, the Claymont-Howard parents became one of the five cases in *Brown*.

Finally, black children in the rural town of Hockessin, Delaware, were denied admission to a modern, whites-only school and were compelled to attend a one-room "colored" school with vastly inferior facilities and construction. Moreover, a complainant's child was required to walk to school every day, even though a school bus serving the nearby whites-only school passed by her house. When the student's mother attempted to obtain transportation for her on that bus, she was told that they would never transport an African American student.

After *Brown*, these patterns of inequality continued, with racism disguised as "freedom of choice"—justifying the building of new schools in outlying areas as merely a response to the population shift to new subdivisions rapidly being built in the western areas of the city (which turned out to be predominantly white and upper class). Left behind were the less affluent, primarily black residents who had little choice but to send their children to outdated and increasingly inferior schools.

Source: Van Delinder (2004).

When I started it was only four rooms, just four little rooms, and of course the hall, and finally they put a room for home economics on the back.

Descendent D: In my case, I was going to the 10th grade. Then I went to Austin (you had to have a certain amount of credits). I was supposed to have been in the 11th grade but I had to sit in the 10th-grade classroom in order to take some of those 10th-grade subjects that they did not offer there in Lampasas. So what I did in order for me to graduate at the time and the age I was supposed to, at that time they were offering evening classes. So I'd go to regular school, and then when evening classes [had] those subjects that I needed I would go to evening class to get those subjects, and I was able to graduate at my proper age.

Interpersonal Aspects of Resilience

The descendents of Quakertown had had a strong sense of community when they were growing up. They had vivid memories of togetherness.

Descendent C: When you said are we getting along together, right here in this part [of town, a] black family lived on the corner. This was all just trees and bushes. White family lived where that dirt is down there, but we all played together and then on busy street, which is a block up, they had a little store. . . . There was one Mexican family—one in this whole neighborhood, it was Mexican Joe, but they're all over town now but then it was just that one family and we all got along. We went to different schools but we got along. Summertime we all played together.

Descendent D: The white and the Spanish that stayed, we got along exceedingly well. We played together, we fought, I mean children do fight, we fought, and if I was at the house and needed discipline regardless, the older folks disciplined the children, and there was never anything said.

Descendent E: The teachers lived in the community. They knew the family background and therefore they were able to communicate better with the children. As you say now, the teachers don't live [here]. Our children leave the neighborhood that they are familiar with and have to go into a totally new area.

Descendents discussed the factors that allowed them to overcome a sense of discrimination.

Interviewer: Were there some things that helped you overcome that feeling of difference/marginalization?

Descendent A: Yes, I guess because I had a good home life. There were five of us, and I had a good, comfortable home life, I guess all the things that could be provided for us at the time. My dad worked at the college. He was a pastry cook out there.

Interviewer: So the comfort of home was there?

Descendent A: Yes the comfort of home.

Interviewer: Has that continued through your life to be sustaining?

Descendent A: Oh, yes. It didn't mean that I had any hate or anything, I still felt comfortable around others and everything, but it was just that I did notice those differences.

Another factor that assisted the Quakertown descendents in overcoming discrimination was their socialization about racism. They expressed how they established "a transcendent sense of identity despite limited opportunities and obstacles to success" (Chestang, 1984, p. 91).

Descendent B: As you said, we were not taught that in my home. As I said, my aunt didn't teach us to hate anyone, and we accepted what was presented to us. We didn't like it but we accepted it and they always encouraged [us] and said, "You do these things and you go to these places and you do these things. Why, it's because of the color of your skin." We just accepted it because we knew that was a fact and we had no problems.

Descendant C: Teachers made a difference. And she was one of those that she didn't only teach at school. She would go to your home and make sure you were doing what you were supposed to do, showing your parents what she had taught you. They don't do that anymore. You send them to school, if they make it fine. Concentrating on one or two subjects, but we got it all. She was an all-around teacher. We all remember Mrs. Hart, how she not only taught homemaking, she just taught you everyday manners and how to conduct yourself. All these things, she just would tell us all these things that would be required of us in our lives.

Descendent E: Well one of the things were the fountains and one the square, and my mom, we were children and maybe some one of us would want to get a drink of water, and she'd say, "No, no, you can't get a drink of water. We'll get some when we get home." I remember my brother when we would go to the drugstore where they had the fountain, he would want to hop up on one of those little stools, and she said, "No, we can't have people on there." She didn't want . . . I guess . . . our feelings to be hurt, for them to ask us not to get there, so my mother just told us not to. Those were some of the things that I remember.

Descendent D: We had come up in it [grown up with it] and we knew not to press the issue at all. We knew where we stood and we never did press it. I always remember wondering why and what was the difference that . . . anywhere we went they had signs up for which way for us to go—arrows. If you got a drink of water they had a dipper that was painted black. That was what you drank out of. Bathrooms was usually around the side. So we never questioned all of that. We just went ahead and lived. There was nothing that you could do.

Descendent A: My dad worked out there [Texas Women's University]. At first when I was very young, he worked at one of the college stores, and the teachers would come over and at Christmastime and the holidays they would load him down with gifts for us, like fruits and candies and all that kind of stuff to bring to us. Growing up you still went through all the differences; they were so many places that you couldn't go. I guess . . . all in all I had a happy life and a good life growing up, even with all those differences.

Sociocultural Aspects of Resilience

As they aged, the descendents of Quakertown experienced changing sociocultural times. They reflected on how they gained a sense of trust and expressed a sense that loss of community was a source of current-day stress (Carter & McGoldrick, 1999).

Descendent C: We had to regain that trust [after Quakertown was destroyed]. But you know when you look at our society today, that's hard. You can't trust the school, you can't trust the churches. Look at the churches. But back then we had all that trust. It's what made you what you are right now, able to be comfortable and talk to us and share all of this because you had all that love and trust and support. We sure did, from our parents, our home.

The school, we got it at school, and church, but you can't do that now. My heart goes out, especially our smaller children nowadays. They weren't taught the way we taught. Children nowadays, they're learning to fight. We fought, but not the way they did now.

Descendent B: Since I have grown older and had a family and experienced the changes, I look back and I don't realize how my aunt was able to maintain a home like she did and to keep us together. There was no man in the household. She was already a widow. Her daughter was married and was expecting her first child, and she and the husband was no longer together, so there was just a household of women. My aunt only had a third-grade education, but she had so much wisdom. That's what it was. I say Godly wisdom. She taught us morals. The daughter that was there taught us morals, so we came up with good morals.

The teacher and the other aunt that we'd visit all the time, everybody in the neighborhood and as you said, the town was small, the community, all the people in this community respected, regardless of the color. We were taught that, and we were just a respectable person. We didn't ever have much, but our house was like the house by the side of [the] road. Somebody was always coming there. Whatever we had, we were able to share, what little that we had. With the little income that we made, it ceased to amaze me right now as to how, but she was a good provider. As I said, I grew up in a good Christian home. That was it, so God was just the head of our household.

Descendent A: I remember one time when my grandmother had come and she had gone to work for this lady that she had brought her home, and she was there and she said, "I don't know

how you people make it and have what you have with the
wages that you make." And my grandmother said, "Well
we just, we know that we have to make the best of everything." I never remember, I didn't feel like we were poor.
We had food. My mother and my grandmother . . . we were
just happy. Sometimes I wondered how [we] made it, my
mother and father, because my mother didn't work, because
she had seven children.

My father felt like it meant more for her to be there with the
children, and she hadn't learned how to make anything, so
my mother was the man in charge. Mother was managing
everything and they kept adding onto the house, and one day
she called my father in and was showing him how much he
owed. He said Lord if I had known that I probably would
have fainted away . . . because, see, she was a good manager.
She could manage with what little money he brought in. We
never went hungry; we never lived without anything else.

The descendents of Quakertown remembered the supportiveness of their families and
of their small town. Family routines and beliefs that contributed to resilience were a source
of pride (Walsh, 1998).

Descendent C: They didn't allow us to run the streets. We didn't go to a lot
of picture shows. All we had was our mother and father, our
grandmother died. I can't remember her, but most of the
time it was just my mother and father. And after they had
us that was all. Everything they did they included us into.
My daddy worked all the time, but every Sunday he made it
his business, Sunday afternoon, that we all got together and
did something that we all liked. This Sunday may be your
time to say what you want to do, next Sunday maybe the
other, but they always spent every Sunday afternoon.

Descendent D: It was a small town and it still is, but as you said in regards
about our school, we had outside toilets. We had outside
drinking fountains at our school. We only had one room
and we had one teacher. Just before I left they did put
another room on and we had two teachers. We had a pot-
bellied stove, that's the way it was heated at our school, and
like the others, I know this. I asked a lot of questions in particular. I was raised by a widowed woman. My mother died
in '32 when I was four years old. Her older sister took me

in, which was already a widow woman when she took me in, which was blessed.

She owned the home so therefore we didn't have to worry about moving from place to place with many people. We took in washing and ironing for a living, so when I got old enough I would accompany my aunt. I stayed in school but during the summer months and every time we had an opportunity we would walk to many of the places to do the people's laundry. Some of them would bring it back to the house and we had the old wooden stove up and the wash pot and the rub board, but we made it.

Mutual Aid and the Community

Descendents of Quakertown were keenly aware of the social supports that enabled them to overcome discrimination. They expressed how they were reassured by and benefited from the mutual aid received from immediate family, kin, and friends (Greene, 2007). When times changed and there was a "disappearance of community" (Carter & McGoldrick, 1999, p. 6), a sense of loss was also articulated.

> Descendent C: Well . . . out here in Lake Dallas . . . we was right in the middle of five or six white families, and we got along fairly well because they knew the whole family. . . . If they had a team or something and one of them got sick, well we would [take their place]. . . . Hog-killing time, they would come [over] and help kill hogs and things. But the main thing, we just had a praying family.
>
> Today we have no community togetherness. A good example is, when I was growing up in my hometown, I had a friend that her mother was sort of wild and she was always catching the train, so we decided to catch the train too. Hoboing like her mother, and we caught the train when it came through our neighborhood and rode it to a section of town of maybe three or four miles, what we called depot town, and got off the train and walked back home. By the time I could get back to where I lived there was a white couple that was coming into town, saw me get off. They stopped and told my uncle, they didn't know my name but my aunt was a real respected widow woman there. They stopped and told her that that girl that you are raising did such and such a thing, so before I could get home my aunt

knew what I had done. So that's just the type of neighborhood that it was in.

Descendent B: We stayed in the flood zone near the poor section of Denton. We didn't have a car, and the Spanish people [had] a car, and it seemed like the flood never would come until nighttime. We'd hear them knocking on the door and saying—my aunt had boarders—and they'd say, "Ms. Boarders, we think we better go to high ground. The flood waters are coming." And they would load on the back of this old truck and we all go up to higher ground. So that's the type. Looking after each other. But here again when school time come, they went to the white school—the Spanish and the white—and we had to go across town to the black school; but we accepted it though.

Descendent A: The Spanish people could go up to the park and get in the swimming pool, but we had to go swim in the creek.

Descendent B: But you know, those were still good times. Nobody cried and said we're doing without, we didn't even think of that. I think we had a lot more then than we do now because we were all so happy and everybody was together. They used to say [it was] kind of a village where everybody took care of each other's children. We knew better than to go down the street and even look wrong because when we got back home they knew it. They would correct us, and then we'd get corrected when we got home.

See I was born on Bell Avenue and Willis and we were one of the last families to move from over there. I think Ms. Ella was the last one to move from over there, and when we were over there my daddy worked at the college too. We had one car and then my mother would go to pick up my father, she would take all of us, and it was seven of us. When we would get up there, the girls would come out and see us and sometimes I'd hear daddy say, "They've got my child and gone. Where are they? I can't go home." And they'd have us all up in the dormitories with them, but we didn't know any better. We thought that was ok, and of course when we lived over there, nearly all the blacks moved.

> Well, we only played with the whites and there was that
> one Mexican family and they called them Tony. I think
> that was his name, Tony, and that's who we played with
> until we moved. Of course I was very small when I moved,
> very young, but we didn't know anything about segrega-
> tion because everybody was friendly. My neighborhood was
> German, after everybody else had moved, and the others
> were all white. In town, that's where you would find your
> difference, in school. And when you would go to school, you
> could only go to the tenth grade. After you finished that, if
> you wanted to go to college, you had to go to Dallas or some
> other place and finish there before you could go to college,
> [if] you didn't have enough credits.

Social networks were highly valued by the descendents of Quakertown, as was the black church that had grown up within a largely antagonistic larger society (Taylor, Chatters, & Levin, 2004). The religious traditions of African Americans have historically reflected the issues of emancipation, enfranchisement, civil rights, and social and economic justice (Farris, 2006).

Descendent E: This is some of the stuff we would have to go through
> before our church was moved in 1922 from Quakertown
> over here on account of Texas Women's University stu-
> dents had to walk through it going to school and they didn't
> want that, so they made us relocate to where our church
> is now, and this is a history of our church, what we went
> through, what we had to do.
>
> We went to church Sunday morning. We went to Sunday
> school. My mother was Christian Scientist. We had to go
> over her lesson every morning before we went to school,
> before we went to Sunday school, and on Sunday morn-
> ings the children from the other areas would come by to go
> to Sunday school with us. They had to go through it, too.
> They were there, so they had to go through it. So I say if
> you come up in a Christian home, you can make it because
> that's all you know, you've been taught that and what else
> you can do. You may stray, but you gonna come back.

Descendent C: My religious life [sustained me]. I mean, I was brought
> up to go to church. We had different activities and in the
> school too. It wasn't just hard or dreadful. We were happy.

Societal/Structural Aspects of Resilience

In December 1921, the Ku Klux Klan (KKK) marched in downtown Denton to intimidate the residents of the Quakertown neighborhood. According to the *Denton Record-Chronicle*, they sent a communiqué claiming, "The KKK stands for law and order. It stands for the protection of the sanctity of the home and the purity of young girls—college girls who are without the immediate parental guidance."

> *Descendent B:* The intent was to move them to another location in the city. Out near the tracks, where they were to move, but old man Miles was about to lose his land, and that is how, that is why he sold it to us rather than lose it. He sold it to the blacks when they were moving out of Quakertown. He got in trouble too with the whites because he was trying to save his farm, so while they were down clearing out the area, some of the KKK came, at least three of them, my husband said. And they tried to burn the first house, and then when it didn't burn it down, but they were happy just setting it on fire.

The unequal schools were a reminder to the descendents of Quakertown of their individual inequality. The inequality of the expenditures on classroom facilities was an indicator of the institutional racism of the era, a time when racism was formalized as part of the educational system.

> *Descendent A:* Well I guess the things that made a difference with me was the schools. We had our own separate schools. We

---

Ku Klux Klan

First founded in 1866, several past and present organizations take the name Ku Klux Klan (KKK) and advocate for white supremacy, anti-Semitism, racism, anti-Catholicism, homophobia, and nativism. These groups, initially founded to resist Reconstruction after the Civil War, are known for acts of violence such as intimidation and cross burnings. They are also known for taking part in lynchings, and some members publicly supported the Nazi party during World War II.

Among the KKK's more notorious events are the 1915 lynching of Jewish merchant Leo Frank, the 1963 assassination of NAACP organizer Medgar Evers, and the 1963 bombing of the 16th Street Baptist Church in Birmingham, Alabama. In May 2006, a KKK group led an anti-immigration march in Russellville, Alabama. Membership in the KKK has fallen from 4 million in 1920 to 3,000 in the year 2000.

Source: *About the Ku Klux Clan* (n.d.).

would go to the other schools to give programs and everything and they usually had a school choir or chorus and we would go there.

I would always notice the difference in the schools. Our school was just one building with a hallway completely through and classrooms on either side. We had the one big heater to heat the room. The big room, just one heater, where the hall was just open at that time and the north wind—the door faced the north—so the wind just went through the hall. In other words, when we got to school (there were no buses, I lived across in the southeast part, and we would walk to school—at that time we didn't have a car), it would be so cold when we got there even though we had on caps and warm things . . . we were still cold by the time we made [it] from that section over [to] this section where the school was. We were just really cold and we just had that one big gas heater and all the kids had to gather around that heater to get warm. I guess that . . . one of the things that really stood out with me was the difference in the school because when you entered the schools out in the other sections of town, the white sections, the building was warm and they had those radiators along in the hallway.

Public transportation was another area in which racism was codified into Jim Crow laws. For example, in Texas a state code ordered separate seating by race on all buses (*Jim Crow Laws:Texas*, n.d.).

Descendent D: Austin had public transportation. Here again . . . that's when I really realized because I knew when I got on the bus that I was to go to the back of the bus and ride the bus, even though I'm paying the same fare. I didn't worry so much about the theater because they had black theaters in the black neighborhood there in Austin . . . but like you said, when you went to the theater there in Lampasas we had to go upstairs, and if it was an important show and the upstairs was filled up—even though whites occupied the first floor and they flowed up into the second floor. If I came and paid my money, I had to stand up to see the movie. So that was the situation even though I paid the price that everyone else paid.

Markers of Resilience

The older residents of southeast Denton remembered the experience of having their community destroyed and their homes moved from Quakertown. The younger descendents had heard the story of Quakertown passed down by word-of-mouth through family and community members. In the mid-1990s, these older residents of southeast Denton petitioned the City of Denton to allow them to open a senior center in their neighborhood rather than having to travel across town to other senior centers. In response to strong and determined advocacy from these older adults, the city finally agreed to help restore an old American Legion building to be used as a senior center serving the residents of southeast Denton, and open to all.

For many of the older adult residents of southeast Denton—who were children of the original inhabitants of Quakertown and who have been through so much adversity in their lifetime—the American Legion Senior Center has provided them with hope, with opportunities for socialization and opportunities for continued learning. They saw it as a vehicle to contribute their time, energy, and passion for life to their neighborhood, where they would feel a sense of connectedness with their community. They were willing to share the story of Quakertown to help others understand oppression and discrimination and to shed light on the asset approach to building community resilience.

> *Descendent A:* Well, they moved from Quakertown the year I was born. I was born in '21, so they were moving. The only thing I know is the old houses were moved over to the section where we moved. They were moved from Quakertown when they moved our families out.

> *Descendent C:* I can share the experience that my husband said in regards about Quakertown because he was a resident of Quakertown and he was a young man, 21 years old when the move had to take place. It left a very bitter experience in his life in the way that it was done, he and his brother, was some of the ones that went down to help clear out that area, and he made remarks about the Ku Klux Klan coming when they were clearing the area over on East Hickory Street. The intent was to move them to another location in the city.

Transcendence and Reconciliation

In 2007, the former residents of Quakertown received an apology from the Denton City Council for the oppressive removal of their families from their homes. Hopefully, this reconciliation will lead to a restoration of cooperative relationships in the community.

Denton Record-Chronicle, February 7, 2007

Local News 'We have experienced a healing'

City Council votes 6-1 to rename Civic Center Park to Quakertown Park

12:02 CST ON WEDNESDAY, FEBRUARY 7, 2007. BY LOWELL BROWN/STAFF WRITER

After more than 80 years, an area of Denton will once again bear the name of Quakertown.

The City Council on Tuesday voted 6-1 to change the name of Civic Center Park to Quakertown Park in honor of the black community that once thrived there.

The city forced Quakertown residents from their homes in the 1920s to create the park in a move widely seen as racially motivated.

"Tonight we have experienced a healing and closure on what was done in the past and the future does look brighter, and we must move on," said Charlye Heggins, the council's only black member. "We can now emphatically say that our community . . . is inclusive of all citizens."

A crowd of people, including a group of Denton schoolchildren, attended the meeting to support the name change.

Third-graders from three elementary schools are learning about Quakertown's history, and raising money to help turn one of the neighborhood's old houses into the Denton County African American Museum.

Source: Brown (2007).

End-of-Chapter Questions and Activities

1. List the inequities in school resources described in the interviews.
2. What attitudes were expressed about this unfair distribution?
3. How would you describe your childhood school and its environment?
4. How welcome did you feel in your school environment when you were growing up? Who was and was not welcomed? Why?

References

About the Ku Klux Clan. (n.d.). Available at http://www.adl.org/learn/ext_us/kkk/default.asp

Brown, L. (2007, February 7). City council votes 6–1 to rename Civic Center Park to Quakertown Park. *Denton Record–Chronicle.*

Carter, B., & McGoldrick, M. (1999). *The expanded family life cycle: Individual, family, and social perspectives.* Boston: Allyn & Bacon.

Chestang, L. W. (1984). Racial and personal identity in the black experience. In B. W. White (Ed.), *Color in a white society* (pp. 83–94). Silver Spring, MD: NASW Press.

Coles, R. (1967). *Children in crisis.* Boston: Atlantic–Little, Brown.

Coles, R. (1986a). *The moral life of children.* Boston: Atlantic Monthly Press.

Coles, R. (1986b). *The political life of children.* Boston: Atlantic Monthly Press.

Davis, R.L.F. (n.d.). *Creating Jim Crow: In-depth essay.* Retrieved February 10, 2009, from http://www.jim-crowhistory.org/history/creating2.htm

Farris, K. (2006). The role of African-American pastors in mental health. In R. R. Greene (Ed.), *Contemporary issues of care* (pp. 159–182). New York: Haworth Press.

Greene, R. R. (2007). *Social work practice: A risk and resilience perspective.* Monterey, CA: Brooks/Cole.

Jim Crow laws: Texas. (n.d.). Retrieved February 10, 2009, from http://www.jimcrowhistory.org/scripts/jim-crow/insidesouth.cgi?state=Texas

Public Broadcasting Service. (n.d.). *African American World: Timeline: Civil rights era (1954–1971).* Available at http://www.pbs.org/wnet/aaworld/timeline/civil_01.html

Taylor, R., Chatters, L., & Levin, J. (2004). Religion in the lives of African-Americans: Social, psychological, and health perspectives. Thousand Oaks, CA: Sage Publications.

Van Delinder, J. (2004). *Brown v. Board of Education of Topeka:* A landmark case unresolved fifty years later. *Prologue, 36*(1), 1–12, 22.

Walsh, F. (1998). *Strengthening family resilience.* New York: Guilford Press.

NEGOTIATING TWO SIDES OF THE TRACK

Biographical Sketch

JM grew up in Hampton, Virginia, a town of about 5,000 people. Because the Hampton Institute, one of the first historically black colleges in the United States, was located in the town, Hampton had a community of "solidly middle-class blacks." It also had a population of poor Black crab fisherman, one of whom was JM's mother. As was most of Virginia at the time, Hampton was segregated, and Jim Crow laws applied (see chapter 4). For example, black people who worked at nearby military bases were required to ride in the back of the bus. JM, who worked on a base after school, remembered being "persuaded" to move to the back to avoid trouble. This was one of the factors that led him to decide to become part of the professional class. He recalled the barriers to education that he faced:

> When I finished high school, World War II had ended, and my father
> had suggested that I enter the military, get the military benefits, and support
> myself. But at the end of WWII the services were still segregated, and they
> already had their quota of Negro troops (10 percent). I went down and tried
> to volunteer, and they wouldn't take me.

With the help of his family and part-time jobs, JM pursued his college education. When the Truman Proclamation integrated the armed forces in 1948, JM enlisted in the Air Force. He pursued his master's degree in social work at a school in the South, but because most agencies were segregated, he went north to complete his field practicum. He later took advantage of the military's educational opportunities to get his doctorate. JM rose to the rank of colonel in the Air Force and became director of social services. He remembered his greatest achievement as helping other minority soldiers receive their rightful promotions.

Historical Times

Hampton University held its first class in September 1861 in defiance of the Virginia law prohibiting the teaching of slaves and free blacks to read or write. It formally admitted students in 1868 during the days of Reconstruction with the mission of preparing newly freed slaves to teach and take on leadership and service positions. Founded by Union General Samuel Armstrong, the son of missionaries, the goal of Hampton University was to provide students with the necessary skills to be self-supporting (Hampton Institute. National Historic Landmark summary listing. National Park Service. 1-23-07).

In 1878, Hampton developed educational programs for Native peoples and established a commitment to a multicultural environment. Susan LaFlesche Picotte, daughter of an Omaha chief, was an undergraduate at

---

Hampton University

Hampton University, a historically black institution, was founded in 1868 after the Civil War during the days of reconstruction. Originally the Hampton Normal and Agricultural Institute, educators taught newly freed slaves to teach and take on leadership and service positions.

In 1878, Hampton developed educational programs for Native peoples and established a commitment to a multicultural environment. Susan LaFlesche Picotte, daughter of an Omaha chief, was an undergraduate at Hampton, and the first Indian woman to receive the degree of doctor of medicine from the Women's Medical College of Pennsylvania at Philadelphia. She later became government physician for the Omaha Tribe. Booker T. Washington, the founder of the Tuskegee Institute, was another famous graduate.

Sources: *Hampton's heritage* (2009); and *Susan LaFlesche Picotte (1865–1915)* (n.d.).

Hampton and was the first Native woman to receive the degree of doctor of medicine from the Women's Medical College of Pennsylvania at Philadelphia. She later became government physician for the Omaha Tribe (*Susan LaFlesche Picotte [1865–1915]*, n.d.).

In the early days, support for the Institute came from northern philanthropists, religious groups, and the Freedman's Bureau. The Freedman's Bureau, which lasted only a year, provided food, medical care, and resettlement opportunities to freed slaves immediately after the Civil War. During its tenure, more than 1,000 schools were built and teacher-training institutes, such as Hampton's, were created. The first baccalaureate degrees were awarded in 1922. Graduates of Hampton achieved status because they later became professionals and merchants and entered the middle class.

Personal Aspects of Resilience

The multicultural middle-class atmosphere that Hampton University provided the community was apparent many years later when JM was growing up:

> We can begin where I grew up. I think that's an important piece, a very
> meaningful piece, to me. I was born in Hampton, Virginia, and grew up there.

Hampton at that time, I am 77 years old right now, so it was different at that point in time, but it was a town of about 5,000 people. The chief industry was seafood, even though there were several military bases around. Now, there were probably two classes of people, now I am talking about the blacks. I do not know about the percentages, but the percentage of blacks was about 15 to 20 percent at most, but you had the solidly middle-class blacks, and I grew up one block away from where the solidly middle class was. That sort of separation was good, in a way, because I had role models right there, but I could appreciate what it was to be in the ghetto, to be poor. But I did not know that I was poor then.

The meaning of having professional status was important to JM:

There was something of a status as a social worker. There were only one or two black social workers in the community. They were black people who worked in the court and could wear a clean shirt. When I finished college, my choice was to go on to graduate school. I looked through catalogs and at that time most schools required a minimum of one year of foreign language. Social work did not require foreign language. So I went to a school of social work. Then got locked into this and thoroughly enjoyed this. But I think that some of the theme of benevolence, helping other people, and being concerned about other people was part of that, and with the church being part of that too. We were very active in church.

Interpersonal Aspects of Resilience

Perseverance and the ability to prove one competent are powerful means of minority children overcoming discrimination (Chestang, 1984). The need to obtain an education, particularly a college degree, can be a major parental theme very early in life (Greene, Taylor, Evans, & Smith, 2002). As described by JM:

Our parents taught us the value of education. And there was no question, that at a minimum, you would finish high school. My father only finished the third grade. My mother only finished the seventh. They were willing to do whatever it took. . . . If you even had an idea about dropping out of school, my father would say, "I brought you into this world, and I will take you out." All of us were geared toward finishing high school. Of the four children, there were three boys and one girl. The three boys went to college. My sister did not go.

Racism can also be combated through proactive socialization in the family. Racial identity and pride as well as cautious optimism were part of JM's upbringing: In that sense, minority children learn to live in two different worlds—their own nurturing environment and the less accepting mainstream society. This *dual perspective* assumes that "every individual is part of two systems: the small system of the client's immediate environment and the larger social system" (Norton, 1978, p. 243) (see Figure 2). *Biculturalism* refers to membership in two cultural systems.

Interviewer: Could you give me an example of any particular moment when you were taught how to overcome discrimination?

JM: There was definitely prejudice there. But at that point in time, you grew up in it. Rather being into advocacy, more or less, it was impressed upon you that survival is the critical thing. . . . So your parents taught this, and you kind of learned. I lived, I guess, with this until I was in high school.

Yes, we were always taught to, and this was not in these words, but don't be confrontational with a white person. And then there were other things, as we talk, that you could use oppression in a way that is beneficial to you. But you still can sort of operate a way around it. This is not an exact version of the words my father or mother, they would never use a curse word or anything, but the essence of it was that sometimes you have to kiss someone's behind before you can kick it. That being sort of a guiding principle that you do have what to do in order to keep going and follow through with your aims.

Teachers in the Black community often served as mentors who inspired achievement (Greene et al., 2002). JM recalled:

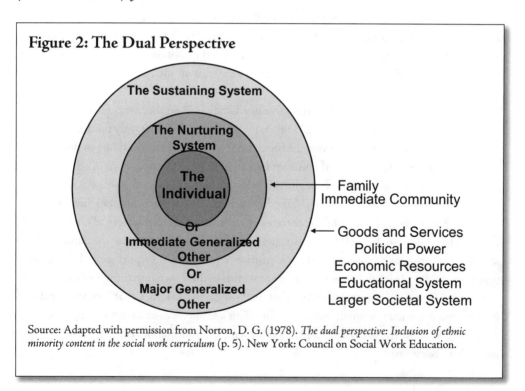

Figure 2: The Dual Perspective

Source: Adapted with permission from Norton, D. G. (1978). *The dual perspective: Inclusion of ethnic minority content in the social work curriculum* (p. 5). New York: Council on Social Work Education.

A critical person in my life, and I thought about this several times going back, there was a Sunday school teacher in our church who was a retired schoolteacher, and was unmarried. . . . I don't know if you know or not, a schoolteacher could not be married. She was a very engaging teacher and took a liking to me. Got me very excited about learning. I always think back on her and the excitement I had for Sunday school class because of her ability to really get into subject matter to make learning fun and interesting. That was about the time that I became more sensitive about the role of oppression that we had to live with as black folks in those days.

During adolescence, from ages 12 through 22, when young adults are solidifying their identity, or self-representation, they are particularly vulnerable to discrimination (Erikson, 1963).

Interviewer: Was there something particular that triggered sensitivity to racial discrimination?

JM: There is one thing that stands out. There was the bus, and blacks had to sit in the back and whites would fill up from the front. I had a job at the local military base when I was in high school. The seats had filled up to a point where the only place that there was a vacant seat was past the back door moving towards the front. So I sat there, in that seat, alone, and a white person got on the bus, a white male, and stood and would not sit next to me. So I determined at that point that I'd be damned if I was going to move. But if he wanted to stand all the way to base, he was going to stand.

There was a black mayor from the community who came up and got me from the arm, gently, and said, "John, come on move back here." Because he probably could have anticipated what could happen. And I moved back. But from that day on I had a bitter taste about having to ride public transportation.

Sociocultural Aspects of Resilience

JM described a special educational opportunity offered by Hampton University when he was growing up. He assumed the atmosphere was different from many of the public schools in Virginia that fought integration well into the 1960s:

Most of the teachers lived in the community or around the community and were very interested in the students. So then after elementary school, our high school was also an all-black school. This was interesting, because it was not a public school. Hampton University had a laboratory school.

Interviewer: That must have been interesting experiment.

JM: Yes, it was. It was given by a philanthropist by the name of George P. Phoenix. He had built the school. It was an elementary school and a high school. So that's where we went to high school. Although segregated, it was a laboratory school for the university, so most of the instructors had a graduate degree. So they had better educated teachers than the white high school. So that was really a blessing that we had teachers of that caliber.

Societal/Structural Aspects of Resilience

The process of development is different for each group of people born or growing up in a particular era. This means that the historical context during which a cohort of people live and the events that occur during that time, such as the Great Depression, influence their belief systems (Gitterman & Germain, 2008).

JM: I grew up at an early age during the depression and my father often was unemployed because the work just was not there. So my mother was often the wage earner. I indicated earlier that seafood was the main industry and the lowest status job that anyone could have was to pick crabs or shuck oysters. So my mother was a crab picker. You can imagine the odor that comes with crabs being steamed. And I used to be awfully ashamed of that. Then seeing a block away there was a physician, or an attorney, schoolteachers, and that sort of thing. I remember longing to live in one of those homes or having parents at that level. But looking at my family, even though we were poor, we were considered the better off poor. I can remember several people in the community who would invariably come to our house and ask my father to help them out. He was seen as a very benevolent person who believed in the people in the old creed of helping one another out. Because he thought strongly that you always should help other people.

"African-American soldiers and civilians fought a two-front battle during World War II. There was the enemy overseas, and also the battle against prejudice at home" (Krause, 2001). With the support of civil rights organizations, on July 26, 1948, acting as Commander in Chief of the Armed Forces, President Harry Truman signed Executive Order 9981 desegregating the armed services. He also issued Executive Order 9980 eliminating racial discrimination in federal employment. These events would eventually alter JM's life:

When I started college, WW II ended, and my father had suggested that I enter the military, and you can get the military benefits and support yourself. But at the end of WW II the services were still segregated, and they had their quota of Negro troops. I went down and tried to volunteer and they wouldn't take me.

Interviewer: This was before Truman . . .

JM: This was 1946. I had finished two years of college at that
time. So my father continued to support me and went on to
school and finished. My reasons to going into social work are
indicated. At that time the draft was in force. You would be
drafted. Since the Truman Proclamation that the services
had to be integrated, everyone was drafted. So I had gotten
my master's in social work, and I had had a deferment or two.
So I knew I would have to go into the military. I volunteered
to go into the military, never with any idea that I would stay
beyond the minimal time that I had to stay. After being in
the military as an enlisted man for two years, I eventually got
commissioned. I guess you can gather that achieving or having some level of status was a very important thing. So being a
commissioned officer in the military accorded me that. Being
a social worker working in military hospitals, I established
friendships with physicians, dentists, and that kind of thing.
So it became an attractive sort of option. Then there was a
good bit of pride in finally getting commissioned.

JM found that getting ahead in the military was difficult but possible. He could help
others to succeed as well:

That's right. It was sort of being someone. Being an officer. It was greater
opportunity that was accorded me before that. There were some stumbling
blocks in the military too. After I got commissioned, I was stationed in various places. But they had a program where they would send students on to
school to get their doctorate. Supposedly, the military was an equal opportunity employer. I applied five times in six years before I was accepted into the
program. This was sort of defeating, but I had been taught to stick with it, and
one day you would get a chance to kick the butt that held you back. Of interest, there were several white officers who had been selected for programs and
sent to various schools. Even though I was late coming in, I was the first black
to earn the doctoral degree. . . . So there was a pivotal point there.

And after getting the doctorate, I kind of got on a fast track in terms of
movement ahead in the military. I achieved the rank of colonel. If you know
anything about the military, full colonel is a significant step. And the promotion
of colonel and to lieutenant colonel was a year earlier than generally expected.
The expression was "below the zone." So this was a rewarding status kind of
thing, too. The bad feature about that, even though the military was integrated,
there was still some things going on. When I was promoted to full colonel,

there were 5,000 full colonels in the Air Force. I was number 36, you know 36 among blacks. You kind of know that something was going on there. But achieving that rank, I started sitting on promotion boards, selection boards, and all of the other things. During those [early] years, I was sort of forced to take things I didn't really appreciate; I was finally in a position to succeed.

Interviewer: So that played out . . . the patience of sticking to it. To get to be a part of the power group. Did you feel a part of the power group then as you . . . made decisions with them?

JM: Yes. It's a significant achievement, about as good as you could if you got to be a general. I guess I got and thought that I would be promoted to general; however, that never did happen. There was the satisfaction of being full colonel and eventually becoming essentially the chief social worker for the Air Force. So there was a good bit of satisfaction in becoming that.

Interviewer: So do you feel you made changes from the inside as a result?

JM: Oh, yes, yes, yes.

Interviewer: Could we hear about some of those?

JM: Oh, if you are sitting on a promotion board, at that time they had a system set up, there would be five people at the table reviewing records of those who were eligible. As one might expect, I would be the only black person at that board. If any black person came up to be reviewed who had a record that was competitive, I would find some way to draw attention to that record. I would just sort of look at the record hard and say something like, "God, this fellow walks on water." And then make sure everyone saw it . . . which folder that was. I guess a lesson, a principle, can be learned from that, too. Even though you are not out beating a drum, if you are in a place where you can influence the decisions, that's really a powerful position to be in.

Markers of Resilience

An important marker of resilience is passing along a sense of social and economic justice to one's children.

JM: A thought strikes me that with my son, I really struggled for a while wondering if it was a curse or a blessing to be able to live in places that were not typically available to a lot of minority people. The Lord had blessed me enough so we have always lived in the better neighborhoods, which meant that my son did not have the opportunity to relate to the struggle and have a full appreciation of the culture of prejudice more or less.

When he went off to college, should I sit on him and say, "Go to Morehouse" or some other place? As it ended it up, we were here in Texas, and he was offered a scholarship that was too good to refuse to Texas A&M. So that's where he ended up going to undergraduate and medical school.

Interviewer: Well I think that you have brought up some interesting points about generational change and how it is different for each cohort experiencing discrimination but not in the same form, perhaps more subtle. So you see him learning in a different way than yourself.

JM: That tradition of seeing education as a means of achieving an end, and enjoying the educational experience. Mentioning that, I can think back, that probably was the case even with my parents and their parents. My maternal grandfather was born a slave and was 11 years old when slavery ended. We used to go to North Carolina and spend the summer there. Even though a sharecropper, he had acres and acres of land, and he occupied the home of whoever must have been the landowner before that. So he was sort of seen as a successful . . . sharecropper farmer. One of his daughters finished normal school and was a schoolteacher out of that experience.

Interviewer: So the determination to be successful began even then.

JM: That's right. We can go back three or four generations and see that. And on the paternal side, my father's father was what they used to call a root doctor. Have you heard that expression? He would go out and gather herbs and other kinds of things. He was seen as the person to go to when you had some sort of medical needs.

Interviewer: This might have been an inspiration for going into social work?

JM: That's right, planning all along what I would do when I get out. That thread could probably fit into the whole idea of achieving status the way you are perceived. Being a social worker is excellent but it is not as excellent as being a social work professor. It was a movement in that direction. Those were the sort of jobs that I looked for. I was blessed with being hired at University of Texas at Arlington where they had a

Integration of the U.S. Armed Forces

Looking at the military in 1940, it would be difficult to imagine what was to transpire in even a few short years. The Army and Army Air Forces severely restricted or excluded blacks. The Army had a token force of four black regiments of 3,640 men, out of a total Army strength of about 190,000. Blacks were not permitted in the Army Air Force or the Marine Corps. The Navy's 2,807 black enlisted men served in the steward's branch (basically as servants), and there were no black commissioned or warrant officers.

Nevertheless, black Americans have participated actively in all of the country's wars. In fact, a black minuteman, a slave, was wounded at the Battle of Lexington in 1775. It was not until the Civil War that African Americans were required to fight in racially separate units. In 1869, Congress made racial separation in the military official government policy. This policy remained intact through the Spanish–American War, World War I, and World War II.

It was military necessity that helped to shatter racial barriers. In December 1944, 250,000 German troops launched a massive counteroffensive, the Battle of the Bulge. Black troops were invited to volunteer to fight alongside white troops. Although black and white troops served in separate platoons, this experience helped the Army break with its usual practice of placing black American troops in separate units and assigning them to noncombat duties.

In February 1948, President Harry Truman issued Executive Order 9981 calling on the military to end racial discrimination. Nevertheless, it would take several years—and another war—before the military actually ended segregation. Three factors would ultimately lead to integration: the growing recognition that segregation undercut the United States's moral stature during the Cold War, the need to reduce racial tensions within the military, and the manpower needs produced by the Korean War.

Resisting the pressure for change was a solid bloc of officials in the services and Congress who held out for the retention of traditional policies of racial exclusion or segregation. This loyalty to military tradition was often disguised prejudice. The military traditionalists—that is, most senior officials and commanders of the armed forces and their allies in Congress—took the position that black servicemen were difficult to train and undependable in battle, and that integration would lead to social upheaval in military units.

The newly independent Air Force quickly learned that it could not maintain its black strength. In 1949, the air staff quietly broke up all of its black units, thereby making the Air Force the first service to achieve total integration. Even before events in the Korean War forced the Army to change, the Marine Corps, pressed to find trained men and units to fill its divisional commitment to Korea, quietly abandoned the rules on segregated service.

It was the Korean War, which began in June 1950, that finally led to the desegregation of all-white combat units. The Chinese entered Korea in November 1950. After six months of fighting with disastrous troop losses, insufficient white replacement troops available, and an oversupply of black enlistees, General Matthew Ridgway, commander of U.S. forces in Korea, requested permission to desegregate his command in May 1951.

Surveys of troops and analysis of combat performance in Korea found that integration reduced racial tensions within the military and that

❖ integration raised the morale of African American soldiers and did not reduce that of white soldiers;

❖ integration was favored by black soldiers and was not opposed by most white soldiers;

❖ experience in integrated units increased white support for integration; and

❖ integration improved fighting effectiveness.

❖ In December 1951, the Chief of Staff ordered all Army commands to desegregate.

Ordered to integrate, members of both races adjusted to new social relationships. The traditionalists' fear that racial unrest would follow racial mixing proved unfounded. The drive for military efficiency later became the primary consideration in the decision of each service branch to integrate its units.

Segregation officially ended in the active armed forces with the announcement by the Secretary of Defense in 1954 that the last all-black unit had been disbanded. In the little more than six years after President Truman's order, some quarter of a million blacks had served with whites in the nation's military units worldwide. However, some forms of discrimination persisted within the services. Moreover, discrimination suffered by black servicemen in local communities reportedly continued to be a problem.

The connection between discrimination in the community and poor morale among black servicemen, and the link between morale and combat efficiency, was understood at the top. In July 1963, Secretary of Defense Robert McNamara outlined a new racial policy that vowed to carry equal treatment and opportunity for black servicemen into the civilian community. He stressed the duty of commanders to press for changes through voluntary compliance. In conjunction with other federal officials operating under provisions of the 1964 Civil Rights Act, local commanders helped open thousands of theaters, bowling alleys, restaurants, and bathing beaches to black servicemen. In 1967, in the face of continued opposition to open housing by landlords who dealt with servicemen, McNamara declared segregated housing off limits to all service personnel.

However, insufficient attention was given to the problem of institutionalized racism within the military and to providing equal treatment and opportunity for black servicemen within the military community. Personal racism also existed in daily contacts between whites and blacks. As a result, racial incidents occurred in Vietnam and major military installations in the United States.

These disturbances continued into the 1970s. The Department of Defense believed that more action had to be taken and launched a study to determine the causes of racial unrest in the armed forces. The result was the *Report of the Inter-Service Task Force on Education in Race Relations* (July 31, 1970), which recommended an education program in race relations for all military personnel and a race relations education board to determine policy and approve curricula for the program. As a direct result, the Defense Race Relations Institute was established in June 1971. But education alone would not be enough, as commitment to change, strong leadership at all levels, sensitivity to problems, and the resolve to take action when necessary were also emphasized. As a result, by 1972 the Department of Defense was moving along a course designed to remove every vestige of discrimination from the armed forces.

Sources: Dalfiume (1968, 1969); Foner (1974); Gropman (1978); *Integration of the Armed Forces: African Americans in World War II* (n.d.); Lee (1966); MacGregor (1981); Nelson (1948); Nichols (1954); and Osur (1977).

teaching and training laboratory for graduate students. So this allowed me the opportunity to continue clinical work and start teaching but with a reduced load to get my feeling toward it. It was a very rewarding experience. And I discovered that I saw myself a major role was to be an advocate for students.

The armed forces has often been ahead of the rest of the country in the field of human rights, eliminating the segregation of African Americans and designating equal treatment for women when many other social institutions have not (Dr. J. H., personal communication, May 16, 2001). However, the "don't ask, don't tell" policy for homosexual personnel (*DODD* [Department of Defense Directive] *1332.14*, n.d.) still exists today, as described by JM.

Interviewer: Sounds like passing along that spirit of resilience involves mentoring others that are in the path as well. I was going to ask if you felt you brought some of that to your clinical work as well, of helping your client to work with you to be resilient.

JM: I am sure I did. When I was trained, there was the separation of clients. And having the therapist here. . . . I always tried to minimize that in various ways. Making sure the language I used fit with the language the client was using. Doing some things that the military did not really like sometimes. As I stayed in the military, I saw that, more clearly, that the military definitely was not the place for some people. It had to be someone who could tolerate structure and fit within that sort of mode. Then in a way advocating for those kinds of people and trying to explain to the commanders, or whoever, this guy, is not just a sergeant. At the same time, trying to move the person towards doing things that would not be so provocative or would more likely land him or her into trouble.

I think of one specific example, and even though I am on tape now and out of the military, they have a pretty rigid stance towards same-sex relationships. I can remember two females who came to me, and they were in a lesbian relationship. By law I was required to report that. I did not, putting myself at risk. But they were still living in the dormitory. My suggestion to them was, "Look, put your money together and go out and get yourself a cheap apartment so that people could not be looking over your shoulders at every moment." And that worked for them.

Interviewer: Advocacy in its own way for the client? Does this make the point that resilience is a collective characteristic? It can grow in the individual as we see you as an adolescent. It also has community properties, family and institutional properties within the military itself. Ways that people can be resilient there.

After JM retired, he continued his activism by working in his community church:

I think the religion is an important part of it too. I don't consider myself being an overly religious person. But as I got older, I have gotten closer to this. Before I got out of the military, the church, we had belonged to a church in Arlington, Texas. When we left to come to Austin, I had been instrumental in selection of the pastor, the new pastor. He has been just unbelievably successful in that church. The church had split at the time he was hired. There were less than 200 people. Now there are over 11,000. So it has just mushroomed.

But the time we were here in Austin, we kept in contact every time he came into town. We would get together and have dinner if he had time or that sort of thing. And his wife, sort of interestingly, [has a master's in social work] also. Now she is about to get a seminary degree down in Baylor. But when I discovered his wife had started a social service ministry in the church, I let him know I would be interested working with that, and her responsibilities as the first lady of the church were at a point she could not really give time to that. As she stepped out, I came in and assumed that role.

It is a loosely structured ministry that, at times, different programs have come and gone with it. One was a senior citizens ministry that now stands on its own. We do Thanksgiving dinner baskets, Christmas angel trees, have clothing giveaways where we collect clothing and give them away. I am also involved with our bereavement program. When I was here, I coauthored books so this fell right into that. So it seems in a way at this point in my life, everything that I have trained for or experienced has really come together and coalesced.

End-of-Chapter Questions and Activities

1. Why do we say that JM constructs his own story?
2. How did he empower the lesbian women he saw in social work practice? Discuss his intervention with them as a form of social and economic justice.

References

Chestang, L. W. (1984). Racial and personal identity in the black experience. In B. W. White (Ed.), *Color in a white society* (pp. 83–94). Silver Spring, MD: NASW Press.

Dalfiume, R. M. (1968, June). The "forgotten years" of the negro revolution. *Journal of American History, 55*, 90–106.

Dalfiume, R. M. (1969). Desegregation of the United States Armed Forces: Fighting on two fronts, 1939–1953. Columbia: University of Missouri Press.

DODD 1332.14: Enlisted administrative separations December 21, 1993. (1993, December 21). Retrieved February 10, 2009, from http://dont.stanford.edu/regulations/DOD1332.14.html

Erikson, E. (1963). *Childhood and society* (2nd ed.). New York: W. W. Norton.

Foner, J. (1974). *Blacks and the military in American history: A new perspective.* New York: Praeger.

Gitterman, A., & Germain, C. B. (2008). *The life model of social work practice: Advances in theory and practice* (3rd ed.). New York: Columbia University Press.

Greene, R. R., Taylor, N. J., Evans, M. L., & Smith, L. A. (2002). Raising children in an oppressive environment. In R. R. Greene (Ed.), *Resiliency: An integrated approach to practice, policy, and research* (pp. 241–276). Washington, DC: NASW Press.

Gropman, A. L. (1978). *The Air Force integrates, 1945–1964.* Washington, DC: Office of Air Force History.

Hampton's heritage. (2009). Retrieved April 10, 2007, from www.hamptonu.edu/about/heritage.cfm

Hampton Institute. National Historic Landmark summary listing. National Park Service. 1-23-07

Integration of the armed forces: African Americans in World War II. (n.d.). Retrieved February 10, 2009, from http://www.redstone.army.mil/history/integrate/welcome.html

Krause, L. (2001, February 15). *Black soldiers in WW II: Fighting enemies at home and abroad.* Retrieved February 10, 2009, from http://news.nationalgeographic.com/news/2001/02/0215_tuskegee.html

Lee, U. (1966). *The employment of negro troops.* Washington, DC: Office of the Chief of Military History.

MacGregor, M. J. (1981). *Integration of the Armed Forces, 1940–1965.* Washington, DC: Center of Military History.

Nelson, D. D. (1948). *The integration of the negro into the United States Navy.* Washington, DC: Navy Department.

Nichols, L. (1954). *Breakthrough on the color front.* New York: Random House.

Norton, D. G. (1978). *The dual perspective: Inclusion of ethnic minority content in the social work curriculum.* New York: Council on Social Work Education.

Osur, A. M. (1977). *Blacks in the Army Air Forces during World War II: The problem of race relations.* Washington, DC: Office of Air Force History.

Susan LaFlesche Picotte (1865–1915). (n.d.). Retrieved June 30, 2007, from www.nde.state.ne.us/ss/notables/picotte.html

FROM GED TO PHD

JOHN GONZALEZ

Biographical Sketch

GG was born in New Braunfels, Texas. He walked to a segregated school five to six miles from his home to the Hubansville Mexican School and did not speak English until he was 10 years old. He had attended 11 different schools by the time he dropped out at age 17 and joined the Marine Corps. He remembered picking cotton and hoping to do more with his life.

In the Marines, GG was sent to a Japanese language school and recognized the value of an education. He got his GED while in the military. After serving in Korea, he earned both a master's degree and a doctorate in education. He has been married for more than 50 years and has five children, all high school graduates, four of whom are college graduates.

GG, who takes pride in his Latino heritage, has been both a principal and a superintendent of education and has an alternative high school named for him in Austin, Texas: Gonzalo Garza Independence High School.

Historical Context

The history of the Mexican American people spans more than 400 years. It includes those who have lived in what is now the United States for generations (since the Spanish colonized parts of California, Arizona, New Mexico, Colorado, and Texas) as well as families who have recently immigrated. In 1848, the United States purchased Colorado, Arizona, New Mexico, Texas, California, and parts of Utah and Nevada from Mexico. The treaty that guaranteed Mexican landowners their right to land was not always upheld, laying the foundation for hostile relationships between Mexican Americans and Anglo Americans (Gonzalez, 2006).

During the first decade of the 20th century, Mexican Americans worked in a number of industries in Texas, particularly the railroad and mining industries of the southwestern United States as well as the citrus and vegetable industries:

> The cost of land, irrigation, and crushing freight charges could only be met by using labor cheaper than any other in the United States. Without Mexican labor, the Southwest could no more have been developed agriculturally than the huge cotton plantations could have produced their surpluses for the antebellum South without the slaves. (Fehrenbach, 1968/2000, p. 688)

Following the Mexican Revolution in 1910, employment became increasingly scarce in Mexico, and employment opportunities in the United States became important for the well-being of Mexican families. When the Mexican government learned that workers' labor rights were being abused, it established model contracts stating workers' rate of pay, work schedule, place of employment, and so forth. In 1924, the U.S. Border Control was founded to patrol the borders for undocumented workers. Thus, the idea of "illegal aliens" began.

In 1942 there became an increased need for Mexican farm labor, as many U.S. men were away at war. As a result, the Mexican and U.S. governments started the Bracero Program, an agreement that allowed employers to hire aliens. More than four million impoverished Mexican farm workers came to work in the United States under the program. When their contracts ended, the braceros were expected to hand over their permits and return to Mexico. Many did not. The program ended in 1964, although the labor practice of hiring braceros did not (McLemore, Romo, & Gonzalez Baker, 2001).

Although many immigrant Mexicans were successful, others experienced prejudice and violence. Jim Crow laws (see chapter 4) and "frontier justice," including lynching, were commonplace. From the 1840s to the 1920s, anti–Mexican American violence resulted in people being displaced from their lands, denied access to natural resources, and politically disenfranchised. These events continue to affect Mexican American/Anglo American relations and trust between residents and community workers.

Acculturation

Mexican Americans have had, and continue to have, a difficult acculturation experience. McLemore et al. (2001) stated that colonized minorities remain in their homeland and are committed to the preservation of their culture while the dominant group prevents them from competing freely for employment and other resources. Because of this history, Mexican Americans experience power differentials that influence their help-seeking behaviors. Goldenberg (1978) described *power* as "the ability to control or influence, directly or indirectly, the conditions under which one lives" (p. 59), which makes *powerlessness* an inability to exercise this control (Pinderhughes, 1989).

Acculturative stress is influenced by several factors, such as a preference for one's language, family cohesiveness, tenure in residency, and coping resources (Miranda & Matheny, 2000). Smart and Smart (1995) concluded that acculturative stress has a pervasive, lifelong influence on Latinos' psychological adjustment, decision-making abilities, occupational functioning, and physical health. Older Mexican Americans have experienced acculturative stress because of the stigma of their history, especially due to discrimination in education. This discrimination often led to fear and distrust of the mainstream system, along with a feeling of being second class.

Four Levels of Resilience in the Life of GG

Resilience has been defined as one's overcoming of adversity and harmful life stress, or as the successful adaptation to a challenge (Fraser, 1997; Lazarus, 1999; Luthar & Ziegler, 1991). One definition of resilience that applies well to the experience of older Latinos is overcoming adversity and negotiating life transitions with competence (Greene, 2002). GG described several transitions with which he dealt throughout his life. In his interview, he shared experiences he encountered and the ways in which he overcame adversity, along with the supports he had in navigating the different social environments in which he lived. GG's story provides examples of each of the four dimensions of resilience (Cohen, Greene, Lee, Gonzalez, & Evans, 2006) and the interrelationships among them.

Segregation, Education of Mexican American Children, and Jim Crow Laws

In Texas, African and Mexican Americans have been separated based on race and nationality since as early as 1820. Attitudes toward segregation originally reflected views about slavery. Subsequently, Anglo Americans extended segregation to Mexican Americans, viewing them as a "suspect class" especially during and after the Mexican revolution.

After the Civil War, violence and segregation were often used in tandem as methods of group control. Segregation was practiced for both Mexicans and blacks in schools, churches, and the majority of public places, including residential areas. Toward the end of the 19th century, segregation was institutionalized and legalized in places with more visible black populations. These practices were extended informally to *Tejanos*, or Mexican Americans who were the original residents of Texas. In fact, a "Negro quarter" and a "Mexican quarter" became features of most Texas towns and cities.

Until 1890, the law required that black schools have equal access to a common school fund; frequently, though, this did not happen. In the early 20th century, conditions in black and Mexican schools remained poor—vestiges of an antiquated educational system. Unfortunately, educational reforms of the Progressive era did not lead to improvements. Many problems persisted into the 1920s: For example, black students were more likely to miss school than were white students; black teachers were paid less and were less thoroughly trained than their white peers; and schools usually consisted of a one-room buildings, generally with a single teacher. The same conditions obtained for Hispanic students. They were segregated because some whites thought they were unclean and some white employers wanted there to be an uneducated, inexpensive

---

labor pool. The schools often had insufficient financing, inadequate educational facilities, and racist material in the curriculum. Because they were not accepted by white society, blacks and Mexican Americans formed their own PTAs and other school organizations. School clubs and athletic teams were not common in Mexican schools. Ironically, as nonblack, Mexican schools did not receive the funding that African American schools did under "separate but equal."

Jim Crow Laws, a complex web of legal codes, were initiated to keep black Texans out of mainstream Texas life. Although none of these laws specifically applied to Mexican Americans, the power of the white society nevertheless generally excluded Mexicans from commingling with whites in barbershops, restaurants, funeral homes, churches, courthouses (for example, on juries), theaters, and numerous other public places.

Minorities, including blacks and Mexican Americans, also faced segregation in the workplace. For example, many craft unions denied membership to black and Tejano workers. Those unions that did exist were founded by African or Mexican Americans and were typically segregated. In addition, there were pay differentials, with blacks and Mexicans receiving less pay for doing the same job as whites. Discriminatory practices led blacks to seek menial employment as gardeners, cooks, bootblacks, and house cleaners, for example. Mexicans pursued fieldwork or other types of unskilled tasks, like construction and railroad maintenance in cities.

After World War I, civil rights activists fought segregationist policies, but significant successes did not come until later. For example, the United States Supreme Court case *Sweatt v. Painter* (1950) required the law school of the University of Texas to admit black students. The *Brown v. Board of Education* (1954) Supreme Court decision declared "separate but equal" unconstitutional in schools, on public transportation, in restaurants, and so forth. Mexican Americans also won their legal struggle to weaken segregation in a series of favorable verdicts from Texas courts. These included *Delgado v. Bastrop ISD* (1948), which prohibited school boards from declaring that specific school buildings were for Mexican children. In 1954, in *Hernández v. State of Texas*, Mexican Americans were declared by the U.S. Supreme Court to be exempt, as a class, from Jim Crow laws.

However, some Texans did not comply easily with federal mandates. For example, in 1956, Texas voters approved referendums opposing compulsory attendance of integrated schools and prohibiting racial intermarriage. The 1957 legislature passed laws that encouraged school districts to resist federally ordered integration, although by the late 1950s, Governor Price Daniel Sr. was ignoring such laws. Come the 1960s, legal segregation was over. Jim Crow had been brought down by court decisions; federal investigations, such as those conducted in the late 1960s by the U.S. Commission on Civil Rights; the civil rights movement itself; and the growing tolerance of white society.

Sources: Allsup (1982); Barr (1990); Calvert & De León (1990); De León & Calvert (2008); García (1981); Montejano (1987); San Miguel (1987); and Smallwood (1981).

Personal

The military was GG's first organized workplace. His military service helped him mature and see other facets of the world. During his years in the military service he understood the opportunities a good education could bring him. He made a choice that shaped the rest of his life:

It was in the island of Tirian. We had gone from Saipan to Tirian . . . I was right in the middle of two different groups. One group over here were kids like myself, they were dropouts, and they were all talking about getting drunk, going out with broads, and having a good time. In this group in the other foxhole were all high school graduates and college graduates. And they were talking about, I remember distinctly, the Bolsheviks. I thought they were saying something bad, and later I found out . . . they were talking about the Russian government. Right there and then, I made up my mind which group I really wanted to belong to: To this group who was talking about getting drunk and going out with broads or to this group who was talking about history and college and everything. I made up my mind right there and then. I said if I ever got back—I was not sure if I was getting back or not, we were still at war—I decided that I was not only going to finish high school, I was going on to college.

So, I went back to Corpus Christi, which was my hometown at the time, and I enrolled at the high school, because I had not even finished ninth grade. I learned that there was a GED program that I could enroll in and within three months, and if I passed the test, I could get a GED. This would get me ready to go on to college. I took the GED and passed it, and I enrolled at Delmar College in Corpus Christi. I was working full time at the Plaza Hotel, where I had been working before, working as a pantry man, a short-order cook. I didn't finish Del Mar because I did not have enough hours. I went on to St. Mary's College in San Antonio, and I needed two semesters to graduate from St. Mary's. Then I was called back to go to Korea. So I went to Korea. I dropped out of St. Mary's University, went to Korea, came back, re-enrolled at St. Mary's University, and got a BA degree. Began teaching in San Antonio. I taught at Edgewood Elementary School, predominantly Mexican American kids. I had 44 youngsters in my class. The youngest was 11 years old, and I had three 17-year-olds in my class.

During that time, I also enrolled at Our Lady of the Lake to work on a master's program. . . . Right before I got my master's degree, I got married. So I finished my master's degree, got a teaching job, and moved back to Corpus Christi, where I began teaching sixth grade. Then I became an assistant principal, then a principal. Then we moved to Austin to work with the Southwest Education Laboratory. That's when I started my program for my PhD. I had gone about halfway. I had about 15 hours, when an opportunity came along to go to Houston to become an area superintendent. In 1971 the

Houston Independent School District decentralized, and they wanted six area superintendents, where each one had about an area of about 40,000 students and about 37 schools. I got the job, and I had to decide should I continue my doctoral program at the University of Houston or come back to Austin? Well, my professor here at the University of Texas, a wonderful man named Dr. Thomas D. Horn, he advised me to stay at [the University of Texas] to get the more prestigious degree, the PhD. So I commuted from Houston . . . to Austin for three years, taking a Wednesday night course or sometimes a Saturday course, working full time as an area superintendent. Eventually, with the help of my chairman, Dr. Horn, in 1976, I was privileged to get my PhD in curriculum and instruction.

Mexican American Education and the Fight Against Discrimination

In 1848, with the end of the Mexican–American War, Texas was annexed, and *Tejanos*—Texans of Mexican descent—were kept at the bottom of the new political and sociocultural order. In a society dominated by Anglos, Tejanos lost both property rights and political power. This state of affairs was enforced through discriminatory practices and violent force. From 1900 to 1930, increasing numbers of Mexican immigrants came north to meet the growing demands of commercial agriculture industries for cheap labor. These workers experienced discrimination in the areas of employment, housing, access to public facilities, access to the judicial system, and education. In many school districts, Tejano and Anglo children were segregated in separate facilities, with Mexican schools were severely underfunded and often providing only elementary school education.

In 1930, 90 percent of the schools in south Texas were segregated. Consequently, the League of United Latin American Citizens (LULAC), a Tejano advocacy group, financially supported a court challenge to school segregation. The ruling of the Texas Court of Appeals, however, was that school districts could separate students using such criteria as language and irregular attendance due to seasonal work.

Following World War II, Mexican Americans accelerated their fight to end discriminatory practices. In 1948, LULAC and the recently formed American G.I. Forum (an advocacy group of Mexican American veterans) joined in a lawsuit that led to a federal district court decision prohibiting school segregation on the basis of Mexican ancestry. Local jurisdictions got around or simply ignored the ruling, however, and de facto segregation continued. In 1955, LULAC and the Forum brought a suit opposing placement of Tejano children in separate classes for the first two grades of school and the requirement that they take four years to complete those grades.

In an interview excerpt below, Ed Idar from the American G.I. Forum discusses this practice, which was finally made illegal in 1957 (see http://historymatters.gmu.edu/d/6584/). In the late 1960s, student protests aided—complementing the efforts of a new civil rights group, the Mexican American Legal Defense and Educational Fund (MALDEF)—and eventually brought about the end of more discriminatory practices. These efforts also led to the introduction of bilingual and bicultural programs in the schools. In the second interview excerpt, Pete Tijerina, the founder of MALDEF, discusses these student protests against discrimination (see http://historymatters.gmu. edu/d/6584/):

Idar: That was the years when, in a lot of school districts, when a Mexican child first went to school, he was put in what they called a pre-primer. Spent a whole year there. Second year, he was put in the primer. Third year he would go into the first grade. By this time he was two years older than the average first grader—they were already behind. That's why you had so many kids dropping out of school when they got to be teenagers. Here their Anglo counterparts were already two, three grades ahead of them. And here they were, so a lot of them dropped out and didn't go to high school. Not only that, but a lot of the facilities in the Mexican barrios, the schools had the textbooks that were handed down from others, maybe didn't have the best teachers, they didn't have the best buildings. And that kind of stuff.

Tijerina: Sometime in [19]70–71, high school Mexican Americans walked out in protest claiming discrimination by the Abilene High School. The girls were bypassed for cheerleaders and various other school programs. Therefore, they walked out and the school expelled them—not suspended them, expelled them. We filed a lawsuit in Abilene in Federal court. There was a firebrand lawyer from Lubbock that came and filed the lawsuit, and we paid him. Instead of helping, he antagonized the whole community. Therefore, I went down there, Judge Brewster from Fort Worth was sitting in Abilene, I knew the judge, and I had to substitute counsel and remove the person. We tried the case for a week before a jury. Finally, we reached an agreement whereby the children were reinstated in school. In addition, we waived money damages—we were not interested. In addition, all of them went back to school, all of them finished school. In addition, the leader, she went on to university, graduated, and went to medical school. Now I understand that today she is a brain surgeon.

Source: *Fighting Discrimination in Mexican American Education* (n.d.).

Military

GG's experience in the military shaped his identity as a human being, an American, and a Hispanic. His love for the country was strengthened during his time in the service. At the same time, he did not forget his culture. He was proud of his Hispanic roots:

> I prefer to be called a human being. I prefer to be called an American. I have served this country. I gave my blood for this country. I was born in this country, and I should be called an American. Although people may not like that, but I think if more and more people do that and more and more people accept that, at the same time not forgetting your roots, not forgetting your background, not forgetting your culture.

> Being Hispanic or of Hispanic heritage has been a great advantage to me and to others because we can enjoy the rich culture of both. We come from a rich culture. Spanish is a rich culture. We used to say about languages that they were to be spoken to different things and people.

GG's military service provided several opportunities to experience other cultures and challenge the views of people of other cultures:

> You have a different perspective on people when you know their language. My perspective of the Japanese people changed a great deal. I spoke their language, and I learned a great deal from this. We were taught in the Marine Corps that these people were all bad, that they would stab you in the back; they were treacherous, that they were mean; they were not really that human. When I learned the language and I spoke to the people, I found these people to be very human, very warm, and very cordial. That changed my perspective about these people, because, in those days, we were taught like in the old Westerns, "The only good Indian is a dead Indian." We were taught that the only good Jap was a dead Jap. But again, understanding their culture, understanding their language, changed my perspective on these people a great deal.

Interpersonal

Resilience theory identifies protective factors present in the families, schools, and communities of successful children (Krovetz, 1999). When at least some of these protective factors are present, children develop *resilience*, that is, the ability to cope with adversity. Benard (1991, 1997) identified four common attributes of resilient children: (1) social competence, (2) problem-solving skills, (3) autonomy, and (4) a sense of purpose and future. Resilience theory proposes that all of these attributes are present to some degree in most people. Whether individuals are strong enough to cope with adversity, however, depends on the presence of protective factors.

Family

GG's family shaped his resilience. His parents, who were not educated, wanted more for their children. His father wanted something better for his children than he had been able to achieve. GG's father would encourage him to learn English in his youth during a time of discrimination and segregation in his community:

In those days, my father used to kind of kid around with my uncles that I could speak English. When they came to visit us, which was rare, he would call me in and say, "Gonzalo come on over." Then he would say, "Did you know that Gonzalo could speak English?" My uncle would say, "No, I didn't know that." Then my father would ask me, "How do you say caballo (horse)?" And then I would stand very proudly and say, "Cabayettes." Then he would say "How would you say cachuca (cap)?" . . . And I would say, "Cacachettes?" . . . At that time, they thought I was speaking English.

But there were other forms of discrimination and segregation. I guess that was the way of life. One of the things they used to always say was, "Así lo quizo Dios" ("God intended it to be this way"); "La pobresa dios le amo" ("God loves the poor"). That meant that it was okay to be poor, because God loved it. But that didn't help us very much in overcoming discrimination or segregation. I think you had to have some aggressiveness or some competitiveness of wanting to do more. I remember picking cotton and looking at those long rows of cotton. I would think to myself, there has got to be a better way to making a living.

My father never went to school. Not even in Mexico. Not even in the United States. They always wanted us, the children, to become better than they were, though most of my brothers and sisters never finished elementary school. One of the things that really, really helped, like I said, I always wanted more than what my parents had. And then I joined the Marine Corps, and that is what opened my eyes for a better future.

Learning had special meaning for GG, particularly learning the English language. At a young age he realized that communicating in English was important. The meaning he attached to the language was significant throughout his childhood:

There was an old ice cream parlor in New Braunfels. Most of the kids, when it was time to go from the farm to town, we went and ate a quart of ice cream. The place . . . I remember was called La Mosquenda, the Fly Lady. The ice cream parlor was outside and always full of flies. That is why we called it La Mosquenda. There were three flavors of ice cream: chocolate, vanilla, and strawberry. Those of us that went there to get ice cream that didn't speak English, when we wanted vanilla we would say "blanco." If we wanted strawberry, we said "colorado" or red. We all thought we could speak English by asking for a chocolate cone if we said "chocolato." And that meant we could speak English if we said "chocolato."

In his military service, GG found another family. Just like his family of origin, this family supported him in shaping his life decisions:

We became a family. Everyone treated each other like brothers. I didn't find any discrimination at all there in the Marine Corps. We were a unit. We helped each other. We cared for each other. And we knew that if anything happened to anybody that there would always be someone there to care for us.

Values

GG and his wife, also an educator, built a family and a home with the value of education at the center. They aimed to raise resilient children with strong values, and they succeeded:

Been married 50 years. We call it that we have been married 100 years because 50 for Dolores and 50 for me. We just celebrated Valentine's Day. We celebrated 51 years since we got engaged. We have five children, all high school graduates. Four of the children are college graduates. Our oldest is a college graduate who went to the University of Houston on a baseball scholarship. Dolores is a graduate of Texas A&M–Kingsville, it was A&I at the time. She has been a teacher. She is retired now after 32 years.

Our second son is a graduate of University of Texas, who is now an assistant principal in Round Rock. My daughter is a graduate of South West Texas State University, now Texas State University, and she is a schoolteacher in Lake Travis. Our other son has enough hours to have two or three degrees, but didn't finish. He now works as a grocery manager in one of the grocery stores here in Austin. Our youngest son is also a graduate of the University of Texas. He has a finance degree. He also has a law degree from the University of Texas. So we have been very fortunate that my wife, Dolores, and I are both educators. We believe in education. We believe very strongly that education is the key for anything that might happen if you want to call it discrimination . . . segregation. Education is the key. We have been very fortunate that all of our kids have been very much oriented towards education.

GG and his wife raised their children to have pride in themselves and to have pride both in being Americans and in their Hispanic culture:

We always talked to our children as being important. All children are important to their parents. We really instilled in them that we loved them. We wanted to do the best for them, and that they needed to be prepared for any circumstances that would come before them. When you are top, you're okay. When you are in the low valleys, you are going to need some help. Both my wife and I were strong disciplinarians. We are strong religious people. We believed strongly in justice. We believe strongly in education. So, we tried to prepare our kids for the good things, but also the things that probably might not be as good. We never did really emphasize that you are going to be discriminated. You were going to be the best that you can be. And because you are going to be the best you can be, you are going to be okay, you're going to survive. We taught our kids not only to survive but to make a good example of the life they are going to lead. We led through good example. We never did conduct a pity party. I never have complained that I was discriminated. No, because of that, if you are knocked down you are going to get up, and you are going to go further and further as you can. We never said, "Poor us. We were discriminated." We never did talk about that.

Sociocultural

Being a role model, being an educator, and leading by example have held special meanings for GG throughout his career. GG and his wife strived to be model citizens and lead by example for their family, neighborhood, and community. Being a role model and an educator fueled his resilience throughout his life:

> My wife and I always tried to live the life of example, to be model citizens, to be a good example for people in life to follow us. I think that through life experiences of being who I am, that I was able to hopefully go through a process of helping people. I have always been able to help people. I strongly believed that God has put me on this earth to do good. That I have believed always. Through my experiences of being discriminated I knew how it felt, so I would not want other people to feel the same way. We are models to other people. The way we lived, they way we dressed, the way we did everything. We were just helpful. We always tried to lend a helping hand to those who were less fortunate than we were. We have been very fortunate that God has been good to us, and we want to do the same thing for other people, to achieve and to be successful to reach the very limit of their potential.

As an educator, he motivated students to have goals and ambition. He taught students to think about more than just today, to think about the future:

> Always let them know not to be a phony, to be honest with themselves always. To have that ambition, to have that burning desire, to have that goal to be somebody, that they are special. They are somebody. They were born to be somebody. The reason I tell people that they were born to be somebody is because God didn't make any junk. If you can do that and help these young people who are just beginning to understand who they are, what are their goals, and what they want to be. What do you want to be five years from now? Ten years from now? What do they expect from life? What do you expect out of life? What will be your contribution?

GG understood the opportunity that he had to motivate students. He understood he was more than a teacher. He was a salesman, a preacher, a motivator:

> Their parents can leave them money, leave them cars, and that will be gone. If their parents can leave them a good education, that will stay with them for life. I used to say I sell education. I preach education. Education is the key.

Some people say let's go into politics, economics. You can't have any of those
two without education. Education, education is the key.

During his work as an educator and an administrator, he worked in schools and school
districts that needed help and direction. GG took these challenges head-on:

I served in several school districts as a teacher, an assistant principal, and
a principal and every job that I had I enjoyed doing—working with the children, working with the teachers, working with the public, the community.
Hopefully my contributions through those people that I worked with will
become something they can be proud of. Always led by example.

Structural

GG discussed instances in which he experienced discrimination and segregation. The school
he attended was segregated, as was his community. GG fought through several adversities
such as experiencing segregation in school and in the community, speaking only Spanish, and
experiencing discrimination from businesses in his community.

School

GG was born in New Braunfels, Texas, a primarily German community. The school he
attended was separate from the larger school. He described it as follows:

I went to Hubansville Mexican School. It was a one-room schoolhouse.
It had two outhouses—one for the girls and one for the boys. We had a
potbelly stove in the middle of the room and a big bucket of water with one
dipper, where everybody could drink. . . . The Anglo kids, German kids, went
to a school up the hill, a separate school. We walked about five to six miles to
school. We talk about busing kids to school these days. Most of the kids who
went there at that time were related to us or lived in the farm communities. I
guess the dropout rate at that time was very high for Hispanic kids. My recol-
lection of being there was that we had one teacher [who] taught eight grades.

GG told of the time his teacher had a problem understanding his full name. His first
name is similar to the Spanish last name Gonzales:

"My first name is Gonzalo, and my last name is Garza." "How do you
spell Gonzalo?" "Gonzalo G-O-N-Z-A-L-O Gonzalo." "Is that Gonzalos?"
"No, Gonzalo." "Okay, fine." Once the teacher got it straight that my first
name was Gonzalo and my last name was Garza, then she would say, "Okay,
what is your middle name?" In the Spanish custom, you take your mother's
maiden name as your middle name. That's where the problem began, because
my mother's maiden name was Gonzales, so the teacher again would get all
confused. You told me that your name was Gonzalo, now you tell me it is
Gonzales. We would go over that over and over again. This is why we name
all of our kids names that could be English or Spanish. We named our oldest
Charles (Carlos); the other is named Louis (Luis); Patricia (Patricia [Spanish

pronunciation]) or Patsy; Laurence, our third son, the only [one] who has my middle name, Gonzalo, but he uses Larry. Then we have David (or David [Spanish pronunciation]). We named them so that they would not have to go through the trauma I went through. Since that time, I get different correspondence from everywhere. I have a list here of about 85 different ways that they have misspelled my name. My name is Gonzalo Garza. I have one here that is addressed to me as "Mr. Greg Garzinski." Then from there on it goes to Garcia, Gonzolo, Gonzala, everything, 85 different ways. This is why in school a lot of my friends changed their names to English names, and I can understand that. Alfonzo became Al, Ricardo became Rick, Antonio became Tony. But what do you do with Gonzalo? Gazi, GG, whatever. I could not Anglicize my name. But even today, on the phones particularly, the way I Anglicize my name is "Gonzalo Garza" [strict English pronunciation]. In Spanish you would say "Gonzalo Garza" [Spanish pronunciation]. It comes out Gonzalo Garcia. So that's the many different ways they spell my name.

English Only

During his time in elementary school, speaking Spanish was not allowed. It being their first language, many students were inclined to speak Spanish. The parents of these young people did not usually speak English. GG described the sociopolitical environment of the time with regard to bilingual education versus English only:

You know some of these schools would refer youngsters for speaking Spanish in school. I remember one youngster one time was sent to the office because he did not have a pencil. He did not have a pencil to write, so he turned over to his friend and said, "Traes un lapiz?" (Do you have a pencil?). So the teacher sent him to the office. This particular school, this was done in 1967 in a school in San Antonio, Texas, where it was a formal written letter to the parents that probably could not speak English. My parents could not speak English, so this letter would have not done them any good. They wouldn't have understood it. In some cases, these kids were being punished for speaking Spanish. This was a long, long thing. They go on to say, "Spanish is a beautiful language," and they have no objection. They go on to say, "The school has always recognized the importance of promoting the use of good English." We have always promoted the use of good English. How can you begin in school when you don't know the language? You have to start with what you know and go to what you don't know.

There were many instances where you could not speak Spanish. It was because of the attitude that some people had. There were some people in politics who really objected to the use of foreign language. Way back when they were trying to introduce a foreign language curriculum in the schools. We had a person in public office that was a governor, or a governess, at that time that objected to the use of foreign language in school to the point where she was quoted as saying "If English was good enough for Jesus Christ, it ought to be good enough for our kids."

Segregation

GG also described the discrimination in the community. He was not allowed to go to the movies or to go into some stores to buy candy:

> Well, we were segregated. Not only were we segregated, we were also dis-criminated against. Most of the business establishments did not allow, for example, Hispanic kids or what we were called at that time, Mexican kids. The theater dis-criminated against Mexicans kids. Some of the stores did not admit Mexicans.

GG also described being segregated on a farm and the dreams that he and others did not have. GG talked about having no dreams of finishing high school, much less attending college. He knew his future was not on the farm:

> In those days I don't remember anybody because we were so isolated from everybody, living on a farm. There were some people who were perhaps bet-ter educated than we were. Most people did not have the dream of finishing high school or go[ing] on to college. Not very many of us who attended those schools even finished elementary school, much less high school.

> I am a dropout. I dropped out of junior high school. I was 17 years old when I dropped out. I had already attended 11 different schools and was in the ninth grade at 17 years old, and I knew that I did not have a future. So, the war came along, World War II, and that's when I joined the Marine Corps. And again, I owe a lot to the Marine Corps because it did open up my eyes to a lot of people who were better educated than myself. I promised myself if I ever got back that I would finish high school and go on to college. Finally, I got back and took the GED. I am a GED graduate. I tell people that my first degree was a GED and my last degree was a PhD.

Activism

GG helped build communities and shaped neighborhoods as an educator and administrator. Neighborhoods are capable of being resilient when they are organized to supply resources, assist in socializing children to the norms for behavior, and provide opportunities for people to get involved (Benard, 1991). GG was at the forefront of his neighborhoods in helping to build community.

GG's legacy is a legacy of resilience. He wrote his memoirs, which were published before this interview. GG also prepared his epitaph for his plot at the state cemetery:

> We have already prepared ourselves a plot at the state cemetery. The epitaph on mine is "Gonzalo Garza—A Great American Pasó por Aqui." In other words, "A Great American Passed through Here." That's the thing I would like for what those kids to understand is that they passed somebody through here and made a contribution, did something good for society, something good for people.

GG was an educator all his life. He continues to be an educator in his retirement and often visits the high school that bears his name. He made a number of contributions to his schools and to neighborhoods in which he worked and lived:

> I have always said that education is not a destination. It's a journey, and we are always en route. It never stops. I belong to Rotary. I am still involved. I belong to the crime commission. I belong to Neighborhood Longhorns in Austin. I still participate in community programs where I can hopefully be some help. I have always tried to be involved not only with the school, but the whole community, the total community programs. I've been involved with crime prevention, Girl Scouts, Boy Scouts, Community Action . . . everything . . . Red Cross. Anything you can imagine I have been involved with, almost every board you can imagine. I have always felt that I would make a contribution to them.

The role model that he became as an educator, a proud American, and a human being allowed him to inspire others in countless ways:

> You know, everywhere I been, when I left the programs someone in the community or someone on the teacher's staff or some student, someone would always write a poem or an ode to Gonzalo Garza. I can feel very privileged that it worked out that way. Hopefully it turned out that way because I was sincere; I was helpful, that I made every effort to bring things to life.

As part of the interview, the interviewer and GG took a drive to visit the high school bearing his name. As they walked into the school unannounced, it did not take long for word to get around campus. They were greeted by the first principal of Gonzalo Garza Independence High School, Vicky Baldwin. She shared her thoughts on the success of the school and its students:

> Let's say that the namesake has a lot to do with it. I was telling Dr. Garza, a few weeks ago, that even though we have students who come in here all the time, they immediately know him, revere him, and recognize him for his achievements. And he stands as a role model for every kid for what he has achieved. When he comes in, they all say, "Huh, there's Dr. Garza."

End-of-Chapter Questions and Activities

1. What role did the military play in enhancing social and economic justice in GG's life?
2. How did he become more self-aware of his prejudice against the Japanese?
3. How did his educational aspirations relate to his achievement of social and economic justice?
4. Use the "Educational Disparities and the Generational Slowing of Mexican American Integration" box to write a summary of what progress has been made in providing education to Mexican American children.
5. Which societal structures/institutions have presented barriers and opportunities in your own life?

References

Allsup, C. (1982). *The American G.I. Forum: Origins and evolution* (Monograph No. 6). Austin: University of Texas Center for Mexican American Studies.

Barr, A. (1990). *Black Texans: A history of negroes in Texas, 1528–1971.* Austin, TX: Jenkins.

Benard, B. (1991). *Fostering resilience in kids: Protective factors in the family, school and community.* Portland, OR: Northwest Regional Educational Library.

Benard, B. (1997). *Turning it around for all youth: From risk to resilience* (ERIC Clearinghouse on Urban Education, Institute for Urban and Minority Education, No. 126). Retrieved January 2, 2009, from www.eric.ed.gov/ERICDocs/data/ericdocs2sql/content_storage_01/0000019b/80/14/ff/1b.pdf

Calvert, R. A., & De León, A. (1990). *The history of Texas.* Arlington Heights, IL: Harlan Davidson.

Cohen, H. L., & Greene, R. R. (2005). Older adults who overcame oppression. *Families in Society, 87,* 1–8.

De León, A., & Calvert, R. (2008). *Segregation.* Retrieved January 2, 2009, from www.tshaonline.org/handbook/online/articles/SS/pks1.html

Fehrenbach, T. R. (2000). *Lone star: A history of Texas and the Texans.* New York: Da Capo Press. (Original work published 1968)

Fighting discrimination in Mexican American education. (n.d.). Retrieved February 24, 2009, from http://historymatters.gmu.edu/d/6584/

Fraser, M. (1997). *Risk and resilience in childhood.* Washington, DC: NASW Press.

García, M. T. (1981). *Desert immigrants: The Mexicans of El Paso, 1880–1920.* New Haven, CT: Yale University Press.

Goldenberg, I. (1978). *Oppression and social intervention.* Chicago: Nelson-Hall.

Gonzalez, J. M. (2006). Older Latinos and mental health services: Understanding access barriers. In R. R. Greene (Ed.), *Contemporary issues of care* (pp. 73–94). New York: Haworth Press.

Greene, R. R. (Ed.). (2002). *Resiliency: An integrated approach to practice, policy and research.* Washington, DC: NASW Press.

Krovetz, M. (1999). *Fostering resiliency: Expecting all students to use their minds and hearts well.* Thousand Oaks, CA: Corwin Press.

Lazarus, R. S. (1999). *Stress and emotion: A new synthesis.* New York: Springer.

Luthar, S., & Ziegler, E. (1991). Vulnerability and competence: A review of research on resilience in childhood. *American Journal of Orthopsychiatry, 61*(1), 7–22.

Marquez, L. (2008). *Mexican American integration slow, education stalled, study finds: UCLA report charts Chicano experience over four decades.* Retrieved February 24, 2009, from http://newsroom.ucla.edu/portal/ucla/ucla-study-of-four-generations-46372.aspx

McLemore, S. D., Romo, H., & Gonzalez Baker, S. (2001). *Racial and ethnic relations in America* (6th ed.). Boston: Allyn & Bacon.

Miranda, A. O., & Matheny, K. B. (2000). Socio-psychological predictors of acculturative stress among Latino adults. *Journal of Mental Health Counseling, 22,* 306–317.

Montejano, M. (1987). *Anglos and Mexicans in the making of Texas, 1836–1986.* Austin: University of Texas Press.

Pinderhughes, E. (1989). *Understanding race, power, ethnicity, and power: The key to efficacy in clinical practice.* New York: Free Press.

San Miguel, G. Jr. (1987). *"Let all of them take heed": Mexican Americans and the campaign for educational equality in Texas.* Austin: University of Texas Press.

Smallwood, J. (1981). *Time of hope, time of despair: Black Texans during Reconstruction.* London: Kennikat.

Smart, J. F., & Smart, D. W. (1995). Acculturative stress: The experience of the Hispanic immigrant. *Counseling Psychologist, 23,* 25–42.

Educational Disparities and the Generational Slowing of Mexican American Integration

A UCLA study, released in a Russell Sage Foundation book titled *Generations of Exclusion: Mexican Americans, Assimilation, and Race*, provides a report on the integration of Mexican Americans. The report's demographic information suggests that second-, third-, and fourth-generation Mexican Americans speak English fluently and are increasingly Protestant, and some may even vote for Republican political candidates. It is still the case, however, that many later generation Mexican Americans do not graduate from college and continue to live in majority Hispanic neighborhoods. Most of them marry other Hispanics, and they think of themselves as "Mexican" or "Mexican American." With such findings, the report concludes that, unlike the descendants of European immigrants to the United States, Mexican Americans are not fully integrated by the third or fourth generation.

UCLA sociologists Edward E. Telles and Vilma Ortiz, the book's authors, explored different indicators of integration among Mexican Americans in Los Angeles and San Antonio, Texas: educational achievement, economic prosperity, language proficiency, residential integration, racial intermarriage, ethnic identity, and political involvement, among others. They found that Mexican Americans are assimilating very well linguistically—nearly all, by the second generation, are proficient in English—but that integration, particularly in the Southwest, has been hampered by rigid institutional structures, ongoing discrimination, harsh immigration policies, and continued reliance on cheap Mexican labor.

Generations of Exclusion revisits the findings of a mid-1960s UCLA study by Leo Grebler, Joan Moore, and Ralph Guzman, *The Mexican American People*, the first in-depth sociological study of Mexican Americans. In 1992, construction work on the UCLA College Library uncovered boxes with the questionnaires from the earlier study, which had found little assimilation among Mexican Americans (even those who had been in the United States for several generations). Looking over the questionnaires, Telles and Ortiz saw a unique opportunity to evaluate the evolution of the Mexican American experience since the 1960s. With their research team, they interviewed nearly 700 of the original study respondents and approximately 800 of their children, the overwhelming majority of whom are now U.S. citizens.

In her foreword to *The Mexican American People*, Moore expressed hope that a later study would find more assimilation among Mexican Americans. And although their study *did*, Telles and Ortiz were similarly surprised to find that third- and fourth-generation Mexican Americans in their study had not gained more, particularly educationally.

Among Telles and Ortiz's major findings are the following:

❖ Educational levels of second-generation Mexican Americans improved dramatically. However, third and fourth generations did not surpass, and in some respects lapsed back behind, the second generation's educational attainment. The educational levels of Mexican Americans in general continue to be lower than the national average.

❖ Contact with professionals in childhood was related to higher levels of educational attainment for Mexican Americans, as were having parents who were more educated and having parents who were more involved in school and church activities. The educational attainment of Catholic school attendees was much higher than that of public school attendees.

❖ Economic status rose from first generation to second generation but stagnated in the third and fourth generations. Annual salaries, occupational prestige, and levels of homeownership were still extremely low for later generations, largely as a result of low levels of schooling among Mexican Americans.

❖ English proficiency had been obtained by all second-generation Mexican Americans, whereas Spanish proficiency declined from generation to generation. However, the use of Spanish declined only gradually, and approximately 36 percent of fourth generation Mexican Americans spoke Spanish fluently.

❖ About 90 percent of first-generation Mexican Americans were Catholic. By the fourth generation, the number had declined to 58 percent.

❖ Each generation saw an increase in racial intermarriage. Although only 10 percent of immigrants were intermarried, by the third and fourth generations, significant numbers of Mexican Americans were married to non-Hispanics (17 percent and 38 percent, respectively).

❖ Third- and fourth-generation Mexican American adults lived in neighborhoods that were more segregated than those they lived in as youths because of high numbers of Latinos and immigrants moving into these neighborhoods.

❖ Even in the fourth generation, most Mexican Americans self-identified as "Mexican" or "Mexican American," with only about 10 percent identifying as "American." Moreover, many reported feeling that their ethnicity was very important and something that they wanted to pass on to their children.

❖ Third- and fourth-generation Mexican Americans were in favor of less restrictive immigration policies than the general U.S. population, and they tended to support bilingual education and affirmative action.

❖ Ninety-three percent of first-generation Mexican Americans voted Democratic in the 1996 presidential election. In each subsequent generation, the percentage declined, with only 74 percent in the fourth generation voting Democratic.

Some Mexican Americans, Telles and Ortiz point out, were able to move into the U.S. mainstream more easily than other minorities—specifically Mexican immigrants who came to the United States as children and the children of immigrants tended to show the most progress, perhaps linked to the natural optimism accompanying a new venture and an as-yet-unsullied view of the American Dream. Particularly in comparison with European Americans, a disproportionate percentage of Mexican Americans continue to occupy lower class stations, even several generations in. Of all factors, according to Telles and Ortiz, education most accounted for the lagging assimilation of Mexican Americans in most social dimensions. Low levels of educational attainment have impeded most other types of integration for Mexican Americans.

The authors believe that a kind of "Marshall Plan"—one that makes a substantial investment in public school education—could address the issues that continue to disadvantage many Mexican American students. Leveling the playing field with whites, in terms of educational quality and quantity, could pay significant benefits in succeeding generation. The Mexican Americans in Telles and Ortiz's study are, by and large, not unwilling to adopt Americans values and culture, but American institutions—particularly public schools—have failed to integrate them as thoroughly or enthusiastically as they have immigrants from Europe.

Source: Marquez (2008).

ABANDONING HWA-BYUNG

YOUJUNG LEE

Biographical Sketch

JS, a college graduate, grew up in South Korea, where he became a successful businessman. He immigrated to the United States at 35 years of age to start an import–export business. When his business failed, he worked his way up from the bottom, starting as a house painter and striving for excellence in each endeavor.

JS had never experienced discrimination in South Korea and was surprised and hurt when he was discriminated against when he sought housing in the United States. He attributed his loss in a legal battle over a car accident in a small southern town to the perception that he was an outsider. For some years he suffered from *Hwa-byung*, or anger disease, until he felt that Christian love enabled him to think more positively. He believes in retaining his Korean culture by maintaining his native language in his home. Although he once believed that his children should only marry within the Korean community, his pursuit of Korean sons-in-law eventually proved unnecessary.

Historical and Asian Cultural Context

Heterogeneity among Asian Americans

Understanding the heterogeneity among immigrant families is essential. Historical and political considerations are important to understanding the differences within ethnic groups of Asian immigrants. The generations who lived through war—such as the Japanese, Koreans, and the Vietnamese—suffer war-related traumas and unresolved family conflicts. Immigrant families who came to the United States for formal education or professional training are different from those who immigrated due to unfavorable economic or political circumstances. Immigrant families can vary by level of formal U.S. education and/or level and source of income. Higher levels of education and income are associated with greater, more positive acculturation (Mui & Kang, 2006).

The history of Korean immigration to the United States can be divided into three phases: (a) the early phase, involving immigrants who came to Hawaii seeking jobs on plantations; (b) post-Korean War immigration (1951–1964), involving Korean women marrying U.S. soldiers, adopted Korean War orphans, and some students and professionals; and (c) the immigration of large numbers of families subsequent to passage of the Immigration Act of 1965 (Hurh, 1998). The 2000 U.S. Census counted 1,076,872 Korean Americans (U.S. Census Bureau, 2002); according to Yu and Choe (2003), 19.91 percent of Korean Americans are self-employed, with a median household income of $42,010.

Acculturation

When an immigrant enters a new country, a certain level of acculturation is inevitable. *Acculturation* is the process of adopting or acquiring the language, customs, and values, and so on of a dominant or alternative culture (Skinner, 2002). Skinner suggested that acculturation as a bicultural phenomenon is more applicable to a multicultural society because people retain aspects of their original cultures while they adopt aspects of the alternative culture. The multidimensional acculturation strategies model proposed by Berry (1997) holds that one's acculturation to a dominant society does not imply his or her detachment from the original culture, thus leaving open the possibility of cultural pluralism.

The four strategies in Berry's (1997) model are *assimilation* (not wanting to maintain the original cultural identity and instead pursuing daily interaction with other cultures); *segregation/separation* (placing value on the original culture and at the same time wanting to avoid interaction with other cultures); *integration* (maintaining the original culture while pursuing daily interactions with other cultures); and *marginalization* (having little interest in maintaining the original culture or pursuing interactions with other cultures). JS is clearly an immigrant who integrated, because he retained his Korean culture in the United States while actively interacting with people from different cultures.

Acculturation Stress

The constant daily stresses as a result of acculturation due to immigration cannot be ignored. Immigrants at risk for acculturation stress might feel as if they are caught between two cultures. They can experience discrimination as well as language and economic difficulties. Lack of acceptance of the dominant culture and loss of family ties and ties to one's country of origin can cause acculturation stress (Hovey, 2000; Mui & Kang, 2006). Depression is a common symptom appearing in people suffering from immigration stresses (Aroian & Norris, 2000; S. Kim & Lew, 1994). Acculturation stress can manifest as confusion, anxiety, feelings of alienation, and psychosomatic symptoms (B. S. Kim, Brenner, Liang, & Asay, 2003).

Despite acculturation stress, many immigrant families still maintain bicultural perspectives. For example, many Korean parents who are invited by their children to the United

States prefer living separately from their married children while maintaining a close relationship with them (S. Kim & Kim, 2001; Pyke, 2000). S. Kim and Kim described this new phenomenon as "intimacy at a distance." Korean American adult children can practice both Korean and American cultural traits within the terms of this new relationship.

Children and youths of immigrant families also say that they benefit from friends and family who share similar cultural values and backgrounds. The support from those networks is a core component of being *bicultural*, or meeting the demands of two different cultures successfully in a foreign country (LaFromboise, Coleman, & Gerton, 1993). B. S. Kim et al.'s (2003) qualitative study of the adaptation experiences of young Asian Americans highlighted the importance of support from similar cultural backgrounds and of connections to one's original culture. People who are bicultural identify with two cultures: their original culture and the host culture. For them, maintaining their original culture and speaking with accented English are not barriers. Young immigrants have bicultural competence and act as cultural brokers in their families, connecting two distinct cultures and generations.

Familism and Filial Piety

Familism is a common cultural factor across immigrant families. *Familism* is defined as "the perceived strength of family bonds and sense of loyalty to family" (Luna et al., 1996, p. 267). In Asian culture, which values collectivism more than individualism, familism is a significant factor determining family dynamics. The phenomenon of familism as a protective factor buffering the effects of risk and enhancing adaptation to culture is common in many other minority cultures in the United States (Bullock, Crawford, & Tennstedt, 2003). The familism of minority families often makes these families uncomfortable disclosing sensitive issues and seeking help outside the family (Dilworth-Anderson, Williams, & Gibson, 2002).

China and many other East Asian countries have been influenced by Confucian ideology (Yao, 2000). *Confucianism* refers to "the tradition and doctrine of *literati* scholars. In fact, it is more than the values of a group of people. It contains a sociopolitical program, an ethical system, and a religious tradition" (Yao, 2000, p. 31). From the perspective of Confucianism, human beings are regarded as "part of natural order and the natural state. The natural state, even for human beings, ought to be one of harmony, not discord" (Ihara, 2004, p. 23). Asian culture has been strongly influenced by Confucianism, in which family cohesion and continuity are important components for sustaining both communities and the state.

Filial piety is one of the core ideas of Confucian ethics and values (Yeh & Bedford, 2003), and it is a social value that deeply influences parent–child relationships in East Asian populations. Originally, filial piety in Confucianism included ideas about children's responsibility to their parents and guided offspring to recognize the care they had received and to respect their aging parents (Yeh & Bedford, 2003). However, the role and content of filial piety in Asian families and society are changing slightly. Sung's (1995) study of 1,227 Korean adults and pre-adults, who are students of middle schools, high schools, and colleges, identified two dimensions of modern filial piety, namely *behaviorally oriented filial piety* (sacrifice, responsibility, and repayment) and *emotionally oriented filial piety* (family harmony, love/affection, and respect). The research revealed that filial piety is not just about obeying parents but also having affection for them.

Levels of Resilience in the Life of JS

JS's narrative reveals that personality, religiosity, cultural adaptation, and active involvement in the Korean community influenced his resilience in his adopted country. He provided descriptions of personal, interpersonal, sociocultural, and structural levels of resilience and the interrelationships between them. There is evidence that immigrants not only adapt but also change their environments (Fong & Greene, 2009). Therefore, resilience among aging Korean immigrants can be understood as involving transactions between multiple systems in the ecological context, and both risks and protective factors emerge within individuals, family, and/or community contexts. JS's narrative suggests that the focus of attention of resilience on immigration in one's life should be on the mechanisms involved in changes in one's life trajectory or how one's life path is modified. A developmental perspective is essential to understanding the resilience process in terms of coping and adapting to the host country; this process must be viewed as one that occurs over time.

Personal

Despite good education and long periods of residence in the United States, Koreans have experienced discrimination in several areas. JS was a college graduate and a businessman who worked hard in Korea's drive to export. But when he started a new life with his family in the United States, he experienced discrimination for the first time. JS shared one of his experiences with housing discrimination:

When I first arrived in San Jose and was looking for an apartment, I called an apartment office which had a "For Rent" sign and they said there were no vacancies. I called again and they said there were no vacancies still. I felt something was wrong when I was refused several times. "This is strange," I said. So I asked for help from an Anglo female. I said to her, "Can you call the office for me? I want to know what they are going to tell you." They said to her that they had a vacancy. They said no to me but yes to her. I realized that it was obvious racial discrimination at that point. They figured out I am Asian by my accent, so they told me they had no room, although they told her that they did. I could have made an issue of that incident since it was absolutely discrimination. However, I didn't have the time to deal with it, mentally. Because I just needed a place to live; I needed an apartment, so I held on to those experiences. That is the starting point where we are discriminated against here. I think we need to learn perseverance living in the U.S. It would be great if the discrimination disappears in this society, but I think it would be very difficult.

Despite the discrimination he experienced in the United States, JS was resilient. He raised his three daughters successfully and plays a very important role in the Korean community as president of the Korean Association in Austin, Texas. JS is an older Korean American with a strong sense of self-confidence and a positive view of his future in the United States: "Around '79 and the '80s, I was the first one who started the miscellaneous supply wholesale business in San Jose. Then I moved to the Mexican border to develop my business more."

He also recalled some difficult times:

> I have experienced ups and downs in my business and still don't have huge
> success. I just lived and didn't make a huge amount of money, but I can say I
> did all my best in life. I really did and do now. I haven't had setbacks, yet.

Resilience was a personal trait he had had in Korea, and it provided meaning in his life:

> I always try to have a positive point of view. . . . Things can be done if I
> do my best. If I don't know, I can learn. The period of not knowing is short. I
> can learn quickly when I face something I don't know. I can always learn from
> that. I have been positive like that.

An analysis of the interview also shows many positive themes directly related to JS's religiosity:

> As time has gone by [after the trial for the car accident], to resolve my
> anger, I went to church. Otherwise, I would suffer from Hwa-byung [anger
> disease]. Maybe I benefited from this event, and grew with my religion. When
> I think about the accident, there was a meaning that my God wanted to give
> me. Now I think that experience wasn't that bad. Even though it was really
> tough to overcome the accident, I learned to forgive and endure from the expe-
> rience. I lost a lot but I also learned from the accident.

His religiosity helped him cope with his experiences of discrimination:

> I asked my lawyer about the reason I failed [or "lost the case"]. He said
> there is no reason. "The reason you failed is because you are Asian. Even
> though the truck was speeding, and everything else supports that it was the
> truck driver's fault." That was my lawyer's answer. Racial discrimination:
> That was the reason. Later, I asked another lawyer friend about it, and
> he answered that I made a wrong decision. He said I had to agree on the
> settlement that they offered me. Most of them lose cases like my lawsuit in
> small towns. He said it was really my fault to go the court. I realized that I
> shouldn't go through the process. I found that "forgive seven times and eight
> times" worked in this case, and finally I learned Jesus' love and endless for-
> giveness. Of course, no one can learn all of them, and the training process for
> that is a Christian's life. So I practiced stepping down every day and want to
> conclude that it was a good experience.

Interpersonal

Values are transmitted through generations. Children of immigrant families are influenced by their parents' cultural preferences. Even though children are more acculturated and assimilated into the majority culture than their parents, they still adopt some of their parents' cultural preferences and philosophies (Hynie, Lalonde, & Lee, 2006). JS explained the importance of family values in the lives of immigrants:

> My family speaks Korean at home as much as we can, so they won't forget Korean. When they keep speaking English, they eventually will lose their identity. Whenever there is a chance, I emphasize that our roots came from Korea to my family and other Koreans.

JS also disclosed the ecological aspect of immigrant family dynamics as he and his children interchange their values (i.e., traditional Korean values vs. American values):

> We talk about what happened to us in a day and listen to other's stories. Traditionally in Korea, fathers are assumed to talk more than children at a dinner table. I have been changed. My viewpoint has been mixed in the U.S. I had very traditional Korean viewpoint, but I have been changed for 10, 20, and 30 years.

The Korean Diaspora

Although there was some emigration from Korea as early as the mid-1860s, mainly into the Russian Far East and Northeast China, the "Korean Diaspora," as it later became known, really began after the annexation of Korea by Japan in 1910 and lasted through the Japanese colonial period, 1910–1945. During this period, Koreans were often recruited or forced into labor service to work in the Japanese empire. Some Koreans escaped Japanese-ruled territory entirely, heading to Shanghai or to Korean communities in the Russian Far East.

During the colonial period, many Koreans from the north migrated to China because of unhappiness with Japanese colonial rule. After the end of World War II in 1945 many of them remained in China. The population of ethnic Koreans in China eventually grew to about 2 million and they are one of the 56 officially recognized ethnic groups in that country. The postwar occupation of Sakhalin (once part of the Japanese empire) by Russia prevented the return of the Korean minority there. Many Koreans living in Japan at the end of World War II also stayed there in pursuit of better economic opportunities.

Korean emigrants during this period were generally indentured laborers and many were forced to leave Korea under colonial rule. Their emigration could be called coercive and their "Diaspora" a "victim Diaspora."

The Korean War reached international proportions in June 1950 when North Korea, supplied and advised by the Soviet Union, invaded the South. The United Nations, with the United States as the principal participant, joined the war on the side of the South

Koreans, and the People's Republic of China came to North Korea's aid. After more than a million combat casualties had been suffered on both sides, a total of least 2.5 million persons lost their lives. The fighting ended in July 1953 with Korea still divided into two hostile states. Negotiations in 1954 produced no further agreement, and the front line has been accepted ever since as the de facto boundary between North and South Korea. South Korea was left in little more than ruins following the Korean War, with poverty and hunger rampant. Drastic measures would be taken by the President, Syngman Rhee, in order to bring the country as rapidly as possible into the modern era. His first moves were to consolidate power, deposing of political rivals and creating what was effectively a dictatorship.

Unlike the first stage of the Korean Diaspora, the second stage (from the mid-1960s on) has been a voluntary, opportunity-seeking emigration of Koreans to the Americas, Australia, New Zealand, Western Europe, and Southeast Asia in search of economic, professional, and educational opportunities. During this period government adopted a policy of encouraging emigration as part of a domestic population control program. In the 1970s, Japan and the United States remained the top two destinations for South Korean emigrants, with each receiving more than a quarter of all emigration; but the Middle East, especially Saudi Arabia, became the third most popular destination. The Korean Ministry of Foreign Affairs estimated that in 2001 there were 5.7 million Koreans living abroad in 151 countries outside the Korean peninsula. The single largest group of ethnic Koreans, about 1.4 million in 2007, lives in the U.S., a million or so lives in Japan and there are five countries with populations of more than 100,000. Overseas Koreans are very active in forming community associations and they make conscious efforts to maintain a collective ethnic identity.

Europe and Latin America have been minor destinations for postwar Korean emigration. Korean immigration to Latin America was documented as early as the 1950s. As the South Korean economy continued to expand in the 1980s, investors from South Korea came to Latin America and established small businesses in the textile industry. Brazil has Latin America's largest "Koreatown" in Sao Paulo; there are also Koreatowns in Buenos Aires, Argentina; Guatemala City, Guatemala; Lima, Peru; Santiago, Chile; and Mexico City.

With the development of the South Korean economy, emigration from Korea began to shift from developed nations toward developing nations. With the normalization of diplomatic relations between China and South Korea in 1992, South Koreans started to settle in China, attracted by business opportunities generated by the reform and opening up of China and the low cost of living. Large new communities of South Koreans have formed in Beijing, Shanghai, and Qingdao; as of 2006, their population is estimated to be between 300,000 and 400,000. There is also a small community of Koreans in Hong Kong.

Sources: Bergsten & Choi (2003); *Brief history of Korea* (n.d.); Choi (2003); *Korean diaspora* (n.d.); *Summary of Korea's history/background* (n.d.); and U.S. Census Bureau (2007).

JS also shared the importance of supporting new immigrants and creating a safe and secure environment for them:

> I've decided not to say negative things to new Korean migrants. People [new immigrants] lose their confidence when they hear negative things of living here because everything is new and they don't have enough prosperity. Therefore, I always support them positively. "What can you do? If you are healthy, you can do everything. You can clean, you can paint, you can be a gardener, and you can be a pump man at gas station. Nothing is impossible. Even if you have small means, you can have your own business, such as in a free market. Being diligent and having a sound mind are the most important things. If you don't have a sound mind, there is no reason to live in the U.S., and you'd better go back to Korea. If you have a sound mind, the U.S. is the place where you can live. So don't worry about it wherever you go." I also encourage them nowadays. I tell whoever wants to settle down in Austin that "even though I can't give you a job now, I will look for a job for you. So let's wait a little bit. There will a job for you soon." I encourage them like that. There might not be any inheritance for my children, but I can show them that I did my best in life.

Sociocultural

JS's narrative supports the idea that immigrants can be resilient and respond to life stressors. As Rutter (1987) said, *resilience* refers to the positive role of individual differences in people's response to stress and adversity, as well as hope and optimism in the face of adversity. Resilience is not a set of fixed characteristics but varies with how people overcome stress across the course of their life. Resilient immigrants create alternatives to solve problems arising from their cultural gap in the United States.

JS shared his ways of overcoming the cultural gap and acculturation stress:

> When I came to the U.S. I experienced many cultural differences between Korea and the U.S. In Korea, we always wore suit with a tie, but here people wore jeans and t-shirts. That was strange but I was accustomed to it soon. There was a cultural difference in calling other's name. We always cared of politeness. Only older people call younger people Mr. Kim, Mr. Park, or Mr. Lee in Korea culture. However, older people call younger person's first name without "Mister" in the U.S. since "Mister" is a title of honor in America. But I got angry when younger people call me "Mister"; even calling me Mr. S. made me angry due to my Korean way of thinking, and even though it was expression of politeness. It took a while to overcome it. I had gone through very hard times until I felt that calling me "Mister" was an expression of politeness. When I heard that, I just didn't feel good. After long time of being angry, I decided to have an English name to have less stress. I was one of the people who didn't want to have an English name. Chinese, Taiwanese, and people from Hong Kong had their English names once they arrived in this country.

They already had their English names in their own country while working there on business. However, Koreans hadn't used English names yet. Anyway, I felt they were different from us a little bit. Younger people calling my name made me angry, but I couldn't express it. So I finally had my English name, William, following W from Jiwon. Interestingly, calling me William instead of Jiwon didn't make me angry. Anyway, the stress I had whenever I heard younger people calling my name was handled by that. I still use both names.

Racial or cultural discrimination is not unidirectional. White people and men can be targets of discrimination, too. This discrimination, which is less frequently seen in multicultural societies, was acknowledged by JS in a discussion of counter racial discrimination. He had three daughters and originally taught them that they should marry only Korean men. He later modified his views:

I strongly emphasized that the men my daughters would marry should be only Koreans. However, I emphasized it less while they attend middle school and even less in high school. When they were in college they said, "Why not? Why should I marry only Korean?" Then it was difficult to come up with an answer and also hard to get a Korean male. It was hard to answer that. When they asked, "Why only Koreans and not other ethnicities?" I realized that I was doing racial discrimination. Maybe I can be wrong. Then I backed down. Later, my pursuit of Korean sons-in-law just disappeared. Then, my future son-in-law, who is marrying my daughter the day after tomorrow, is American. My persistence for Korean sons-in-law slowly disappeared. I expected my last child to marry a Korean guy, but I am not sure. So-so, fifty-fifty . . .

Structural

JS emphasized the importance of Korean Americans' active participation in establishing and influencing institutional and community structures in the United States. He clearly delineated resilience as a large-scale phenomenon including the ecological context of neighborhoods and the overarching social, political, legal, economic, and value patterns of the larger society (Greene, 2002):

The Korean social worker should help us. Next, lawyers should not pursue just money. If we have lawyers who have social work minds, many Koreans can benefit from this. Frankly, it is unfortunate that there is no such lawyer who has that mindset in the Korean community. I hope there will be more lawyers produced with that mindset from 1.5- and second-generation Korean Americans. There are many Korean Americans who can't say they are disadvantaged, even though they experience mistreatment, racial discrimination, and several other disadvantages. There are many Koreans who don't have economic power everywhere. They just bury these experiences and don't deal with them since they don't have power. There should be many lawyers who have that on their minds from second generation. There was the murderer, Chul-soo Lee, in L.A. in the late '70s. At that time Chul-soo Lee murdered, or did something wrong, again while he was in jail. When the American mass media talked about it loudly, one Korean lawyer, actually before becoming a lawyer, took the case and did great job. He thought that perhaps there was some way in which Chul-soo Lee was disadvantaged, such as in the investigation of the cause of the murder or something like that. The lawyer's name was Jae-kun Yoo. He appeared in the newspaper since he worked for Chul-soo Lee a lot. We supported him when we read the newspaper. There should be more people like him. We praised him and clapped for him. Finally, he did great job. He did excellent work for Chul-soo Lee. He cared for justice and righteousness. He wanted to help others and finally became a lawyer. I still remember vividly what he did in the late 70s.

Social Activism

JS endeavored to expand his protective environment following his immigration. One of the ways for JS to cultivate a protective environment was to have strong Korean associations and Korean schools in the United States. Struggling with several barriers in a foreign country, JS used the protective environmental factors around him and changed the environment on which he is now dependent. Over time, this mutual influence will have a cumulative effect on one's life and will change the total person–environment configuration:

I tell the importance of Korean language to students at Austin Korean School. The children who are grown up here [the United States] are supposed to speak English well. If the Korean parents speak only English at home, their children will lose Korean. That is the thing we should care about, not about speaking English. The child who goes school here will speak English well, so just care about teaching Korean. I always say that. Speaking Korean will help them overcome trials and tribulations. The identity "I am Korean" disappears when one can't speak Korean. We are Korean Americans. However, people forget that and say, "I'm an American citizen. I'm not Korean. I'm an American citizen." I think our appearance will last as long as humans exist. Since we always have a certain appearance, people constantly ask "Where are you from?" even though the person was born here and has lived here more than 50 years, 70 years. Since that is the way in the U.S., we always should keep in mind that we are Korean. When we lose our language, we lose our identity. Language is the first and most important part of our identity. When we know our language, we can love our ancestral home country and want to go there. When we are familiar with it, we can feel that we are rooted in Korea. That is why language is important, and why Austin Korean School is important, along with the Korean Association.

JS's narrative shows the importance of personal traits, cultural adaptation, and active community involvement in his resilience. It clarifies the concurrent relationship between protective factors and his resilience, which is based on an ecological–developmental perspective. The ecological perspective characterizes the attainment of personal well-being as a lifelong process of numerous person–environment exchanges. This is why resilient older immigrants not only use protective factors around them but also cultivate their environments to be protective ones.

Importance of Culture

There are more than 800 Korean-language schools in the United States. Korean-language schools or Sunday schools in Korean churches are good sources of education in the Korean language and culture. They play a significant role as a bridge connecting young Korean American generations to older Korean Americans and traditional Korean culture. Some immigrant students are aware of the stereotypical perceptions that can hinder them from acquiring the culture and language of their origin. Whereas the Korean American society teaches the younger generations Korean and educates them about Korean culture, American school systems should provide institutional support to immigrant students.

Sources: Brittain (2005); and Overseas Korean Educational Institutions (n.d.).

End-of-Chapter Questions and Activities

1. How does JS interact with his family in regard to assimilation?
2. What does he hope to achieve by being a leader in the Korean American community?
3. What is the transformational experience that moves JS from Hwa-byung to a more loving person?

References

Aroian, K., & Norris, A. (2000). Resilience, stress, and depression among Russian immigrants to Israel. *Western Journal of Nursing Research, 22,* 54–67.

Bergsten, C. F., & Choi, I. (Eds.). (2003). *The Korean diaspora in the world economy.* Washington, DC: Peterson Institute for International Economics.

Berry, J. (1997). Immigration, acculturation, and adaptation. *Applied Psychology, 46,* 5–33.

Brief history of Korea. (n.d.). Available at http://www.geocities.com/mokkim/koreahistory.html

Brittain, C. (2005, November). *On learning English: The importance of school context, immigrant communities, and the racial symbolism of the English language in understanding the challenge for immigrant adolescents.* Retrieved January 10, 2009, from http://www.ccis-ucsd.org/publications/wrkg125.pdf

Bullock, K., Crawford, S., & Tennstedt, S. (2003). Employment and caregiving: Exploration of African American caregivers. *Social Work, 48,* 150–162.

Choi, I. (2003). Korean diaspora in the making: Its current status and impact on the Korean economy. In C. F. Bergsten & I. Choi (Eds.), *The Korean diaspora in the world economy* (pp. 9–29). Washington, DC: Peterson Institute for International Economics.

Dilworth-Anderson, P., Williams, I., & Gibson, B. (2002). Issues of race, ethnicity, and culture in caregiving research: A 20-year review (1980–2000). *Gerontologist, 42,* 237–272.

Fong, R., & Greene, R. (2009). Risk, resilience, and resettlement. In R. R. Greene & N. Kropf (Eds.), *Human behavior theory: A diversity framework* (pp. 147–166). New Brunswick, NJ: Aldine Transaction Press.

Greene, R. R. (2002). Human behavior theory. In R. R. Greene (Ed.), *Resiliency: An integrated approach to practice, policy, and research* (pp. 1–27). Washington, DC: NASW Press.

Hovey, J. D. (2000). Acculturative stress, depression, and suicidal ideation in Mexican immigrants. *Cultural Diversity and Ethnic Minority Psychology, 6,* 134–151.

Hurh, W. (1998). *The Korean Americans.* Westport, CT: Greenwood Press.

Hynie, M., Lalonde, R., & Lee, N. (2006). Parents–child value transmission among Chinese immigrants to North America: The case of traditional mate preferences. *Cultural Diversity and Traditional Minority Psychology, 12,* 230–244.

Ihara, C. (2004). Are individual rights necessary? A Confucian perspective. In K. Shun & D. B. Wong (Eds.), *Confucian ethics: A comparative study of self, autonomy, and community* (pp. 11–30). New York: Cambridge University Press.

Kim, B. S., Brenner, B. R., Liang, C. T., & Asay, P. A. (2003). A qualitative study of adaptation experiences of 1.5-generational Asian Americans. *Cultural Diversity and Ethnic Minority Psychology, 9,* 156–170.

Kim, S., & Kim, K. (2001). Intimacy at a distance, Korean American style: Invited Korean elderly and their married children. In L. K. Olson (Ed.), *Age through ethnic lenses: Caring for the elderly in a multicultural society* (pp. 45–58). New York: Rowman & Littlefield.

Kim, S., & Lew, L. (1994). Ethnic identity, role integration, quality of life and depression in Korean-American women. *Archives of Psychiatric Nursing, 8,* 348–356.

Korean diaspora. (n.d.). Retrieved February 24, 2009, from Wikipedia: http://en.wikipedia.org/wiki/Korean_diaspora

LaFromboise, T., Coleman, H. L., & Gerton, J. (1993). Psychological impact of biculturalism: Evidence and theory. *Psychological Bulletin, 114,* 395–412.

Luna, I., Ardon, E., Lim, Y., Cromwell, S., Phillips, L., & Russell, C. (1996). *The relevance of familism in cross-cultural studies of family caregiving. Western Journal of Nursing Research, 18,* 267–274.

Mui, A. C., & Kang, S. (2006). Acculturation stress and depression among Asian immigrant elders. *Social Work, 51,* 243–255.

Overseas Korean Educational Institutions. (n.d.). *Korean education center.* Retrieved December 20, 2008, from http://www.interedu.go.kr/edu_net/overseas/center.htm

Pyke, K. (2000). "The normal American family" as an interpretive structure of family life among grown children of Korean and Vietnamese immigrants. *Journal of Marriage and Family, 62,* 240–255.

Rutter, M. (1987). Psychological resilience and protective mechanisms. *American Journal of Orthopsychiatry, 57,* 316–331.

Skinner, J. (2002). Acculturation: Measures of ethnic accommodation to the dominant American culture. *In* J. H. Skinner, H. John, J. A. Teresi, D. Holmes, S. M. Stahl, & A. L. Stewart (Eds.), *Multicultural measurement in older populations* (pp. 37–51). New York: Springer.

Summary of Korea's history/background. (n.d.). Available at http://asianinfo.org/asianinfo/korea/pro-history.htm

Sung, K. (1995). Measures and dimensions of filial piety in Korea. *Gerontologist, 35,* 240–247.

U.S. Census Bureau. (2002). *The Asian population: 2000.* Washington, DC: U.S. Government Printing Office.

U.S. Census Bureau. (2007). *American FactFinder* [2007 American Community Survey, B02006 Asian Alone by Selected Groups]. Available at http://www.ipsr.ku.edu/ksdata/census/aff.pdf

Yao, X. (2000). *An introduction to Confucianism.* Cambridge, England: Cambridge University Press.

Yeh, K., & Bedford, O. (2003). A test of the dual filial piety model. *Asian Journal of Social Psychology, 6,* 215–228.

Yu, E.-Y., & Choe, P. (2003, January). *100 years of American history: The Korean American population* [PowerPoint presentation]. Retrieved October 10, 2005, from http://www.calstatela.edu/centers/ckaks/census_tables.html

The Making of
a Social Activist

Harriet L. Cohen

Biographical Sketch

JG is a Jewish woman who grew up in the North and did not face discrimination until planning her honeymoon, when she learned that she could not stay in certain hotels because they did not accept Jews.

In the early 1950s, she, her husband, and their baby moved from Florida to Mississippi to start a business. In this new location, now her home, she was confronted with the reality of discrimination. At that time, the White Citizens Council (WCC) was forming in Mississippi in preparation for the U.S. Supreme Court decision on *Brown v. Board of Education of Topeka*. The WCC called for the abolition of public schools, the creation of a 49th state for Negroes, and the suspension of the NAACP (http://www.olemiss.edu/depts/generallibrary/files/archives/collections/guides/latesthtml/MUM00072.html). WCC members knocked on her door and asked, "Will you join us?" She refused. Though she chose not to join the organization, this interaction was a transformative moment in her life, opening her eyes and her heart to the overt racism and discrimination in Mississippi.

JG went on to help establish the Mississippi Panel of American Women, an advocacy group that educated individuals and groups about the effects of racism, anti-Semitism, and other forms of oppression. Although her husband and children supported her work, her children were ostracized because of her activism. JG also returned to school to earn her master's degree in order to further her work with those who were marginalized by society. JG now acknowledges the risks she took by promoting school integration, advocating the repeal of the Jim Crow laws in Mississippi and fighting against discrimination in education, health care, restaurants, and all public facilities.

Historical Context

Major social and political events during the mid-20th century propelled JG into social action. Some of these included Mississippi's response to the U.S. Supreme Court decision on *Brown v. Board of Education*; the establishment of the WCCs; the activities of the Ku Klux Klan; the passage of the Civil Rights Act of 1964 and the Voting Rights Act of 1965; the murder of three civil rights workers in Philadelphia, Mississippi; and the bombing of the newly constructed Jewish synagogue in Jackson, Mississippi. It was within this sociohistorical context of racism, prejudice, and oppression that JG felt called to help establish the Mississippi Panel of American Women. She saw it as an effort to help build bridges between various racial and religious groups and to strive to change prejudiced and intolerant attitudes about these groups, "working for a brighter future and hoping for a better world" (Cohen, Greene, Lee, Gonzalez, & Evans, 2006, p. 35).

Personal Aspects of Resilience

JG grew up in New York City. She recalled:

> I did not experience any prejudice that I remember growing up. . . . And the only time I experienced any prejudice was when I got married and we were going to Nassau on our honeymoon and we wrote to the largest hotel in Nassau for a room. And they wrote back to the travel agent that they would be delighted to have us stay there and they wanted us to know that they did not accept Jews.

JG, her husband, and their baby moved to Jackson, Mississippi, in 1951, where she busied herself taking care of her growing family; she had limited involvement in the community. However, events happening in her world called her to action. Prior to joining the panel, JG recalled:

White Citizens Council (WCC)

The White Citizens Council (WCC) was formed on July 11, 1954, and was composed of plantation owners, bankers, doctors, lawyers, legislators, preachers, teachers, and merchants (White Citizens' Council, 2009a). The purpose of this organization was to prevent the implementation of the *Brown v. Board of Education* decision and to preserve segregation in Mississippi. Although the WCC occasionally resorted to violence, their main tactic was to carry out economic reprisals on those who opposed them. Black people, who were viewed as too supportive of desegregation and voting rights, could find themselves and their family members unemployed (White Citizens' Council, 2009b). The WCC was so successful in Mississippi that it took the state 10 years after the *Brown* decision to implement school integration.

I had been completely immersed in the Temple. You know, and the [Temple] sisterhood . . . and playing mah-jongg [tiles] and raising young children, you know, and things like that.

However, by 1957 the Citizens Council, the White Citizens Council, had been formed and they were going around the state to different localities, door by door. Because I remember someone coming to the house and saying, "Will you join us?" The White Citizens Councils were started by businessmen in Mississippi. It was started in 1954 by a Robert Patterson in Indianola, Mississippi. And it was pro-segregation. It was strictly to promote and keep the community segregated. So when these White Citizens Council representatives came to the house, I said, no, that I was not interested in joining. And then became aware of racial problems that had never really been . . . I had not been active in the community before that.

JG's experience with the WCC and the Ku Klux Klan forced her to confront her personal values, propelling her into action. She demonstrated initiative and an ability to influence her larger environment. The belief that one has the resources and capacity to make a difference is often referred to as *internal locus of control* (Sue, 2006). It involves the ability of individuals to "take charge of their lives and witness the tangible evidence of competence" (Wolin & Wolin, 1993, p. 139).

The WCC's knock at her door was a transformative event for JG, one that shaped her life and gave it personal meaning. As a result, she helped to develop the Mississippi Panel of American Women and served on the panel for many years. She also helped to start panels in

---

Ku Klux Klan (KKK)

Though initially founded in 1866, several past and present organizations have taken the name Ku Klux Klan (KKK), advocating White supremacy and supporting anti-Semitism, racism, anti-Catholicism, homophobia, and nativism. First founded to resist Reconstruction after the Civil War, these groups are known for intimidation, cross burnings (*July 11, 1954: Citizens Council formed*, n.d.), lynchings, and in some cases supporting Nazi causes during World War II. Among the KKK's more notorious events were the lynching of Jewish merchant Leo Frank; the assassination of NAACP organizer Medgar Evers; the 1963 bombing of the 16th Street Baptist Church in Birmingham, Alabama; and the 1964 murder of three civil rights workers in Philadelphia, Mississippi (see Broder, 2005). KKK members were also found guilty of the bombing of the only Jewish synagogue in Jackson, Mississippi, Beth Israel Congregation, and its rabbi's home in 1967. Though the KKK's membership has fallen from a high of 4 million in 1920 to possibly only 3,000 in 2000, as recently as May 2006 KKK members led an anti-immigration march in Russellville, Alabama.

Birmingham, Alabama, and Memphis, Tennessee. JG's narrative of continuity built on her experience with the Panel of American Women. JG explained, "It was an eye opener. . . . I did nothing but civil rights for years . . . and I just went to meetings constantly. It was galvanizing."

She stated that the experience

> definitely shaped my own life, because I went back to school and finished. And then I worked as a social worker in the . . . Catholic hospital there. And then when I moved to Dallas, I worked as a social worker at the Dallas Home with Jewish Aging. And for 13 years [I] worked with families.

JG's actions, based on her own values, demonstrate that "values facilitate the connection between the mundane events of everyday life and the macrosocial, historical, political, and economic context in which lives are lived and cultural constructs are shaped" (Becker, 1997, p. 109).

Interpersonal Aspects of Resilience

JG experienced the support of her family and her friends. "My children never said, 'Why are you doing this?' or 'What are you doing?' They just took it for granted. Right. They just took it for granted." Another source of resilience was provided by her connection with other activists. JG described the composition of the Mississippi Panel of American Women:

> Most of us were probably 30s, 40s, 50—30, 40, 50s. Yeah, not much older than that. . . . We were all active in certain areas of the community. And we all knew each other. . . . We were five middle-class women sitting in front of an audience. And very middle class and all friends and that we had a . . . we had a message and a story to tell.

Through her involvement with the panel she met other people, allowing her to see new choices for her life's work (Wolin & Wolin, 1993):

Panel of American Women

The Panel of American Women was founded in Kansas City in 1957. Its purpose was to increase awareness about prejudice, racism, and all forms of discrimination (Murphy, 1997). In addition to Kansas City, panels were established in Jackson, Mississippi; Memphis, Tennessee; New Orleans, Louisiana; Little, Rock, Arkansas; and Dallas, Texas. The panels consisted of five or six women—Jewish, Catholic, African American, White Protestant, and occasionally Asian American—as well as a moderator (Barnes, 2002). These panels spoke in schools, churches and synagogues, and civic organizations. Each woman spoke about her experiences and how her life and community had been affected by prejudice (*Panel of American Women Records, 1963–1999*, n.d.). The moderator then opened the floor to questions from the audience. Participants were offered the opportunity to learn more about people of different cultures, religions, and races/ethnicities. During its three years of existence, the Mississippi Panel of American Women toured the state, making as many as 1,000 presentations.

One of my best friends was a nun that I met. And I still see her, you know, Sister June. . . . She hired me for the first social work department that was opened at St. Dominick's Hospital. . . . So we got her for the panel. That was basically how I met her.

Though JG was committed to the development of the Panel of American Women, she was keenly aware that her activism involved risk, danger, and a negative impact on her family:

You talked about being on the subversive list. Did I mentioned that they took your license plates if you went out to the small black college, where there was a very progressive black college called Tugaloo in Tugaloo, Mississippi? And they had speakers . . . I remember when we were trying to get the panel together that I had black women visiting my house, which I had never done before. And I remember my neighbor who lived across the street talking to my husband . . . saying, "You've got to make your wife stop. My house is going to be bombed instead of your house! They are going to mistake my house for your house. So you've got to make your wife stop doing what she is doing, having black people over."

JG revealed two examples of how her work affected her children:

Well, my oldest daughter was the one who was the most involved . . . . Because I took her to meetings and took her to different things. She is a social worker today. All of my children, well not all of them. But . . . my oldest daughter is a social worker. My youngest daughter is a . . . she was in rehabilitation. She is a social worker of sorts, not a certified social worker, but . . . in working with people. My son-in-law is a psychologist. . . . My other daughter was an accountant. Is an accountant.

I will tell you this story. My . . . in 1968, the Mississippi Freedom Democratic party was started. And I was doing . . . I was working with the . . . on the precinct level. Going to precinct meetings and everything. And I was asked to go to the 1968 Democratic Convention in Chicago. And my husband for the first time said, "No, don't go. Really . . . I don't want." . . . We were in business . . . and he said, "I really don't want you to go." So some good friends of ours . . . he was the head of the Human Relations Council in Jackson. And so he and his wife . . . his wife said, "Let me take B." B. was about 16 or 17. I said let them take B. And she will be a go-fer at the convention. So I said, "Fine." So I let her go. And then we . . . and then I had never thought there would be any trouble. Any real trouble at the convention. But it was really one of the highlights of her life. Even though when she called, I said, "Don't go out. Don't get involved in the fighting. Or anything like that." But she met Martin Luther King. She has his button. You know . . . she says it was a great experience for her . . . to be there.

And another thing that happened was that my daughter, I'm talking about B., my daughter, when she went back to a high school reunion a number of years ago. She was met by a neighbor who she had gone to school with. And the first thing she said to her, "B. I want to apologize." B. said, "What for?" She said, "My mother made me stop seeing you. And I want . . . that was . . . I'm ashamed that I followed . . . that I did what she told me to do. And I really want to apologize for not being your friend." Because they had been close friends and all of a sudden she stopped talking to her.

Sociocultural Aspects of Resilience

As mentioned earlier, it was not until the WCC representatives confronted her that JG became conscious of not only the racial problems in her community—including sexism and anti-Semitism:

> So, I began to seek organizations and to seek people that I knew who I felt would be . . . feel the way I did. I joined the League of Women Voters. I joined AAUW, the American Association of University Women. I joined Women's Interfaith Groups. And met really very interesting people. The boycotts began in the early '60s. They were trying to integrate the lunch counters. It first started with the lunch counters. And people came to Mississippi, young and old, black and white, from all over the country. Many were arrested. And the fear escalated within the white community in Jackson. Many feared for their jobs. Many feared for their lives. The Ku Klux Klan became active.

> Against this backdrop of unrest, we developed about 20 panelists . . . at the beginning. There was a Catholic woman, a Protestant, Jewish, black, and the moderator. The Jewish person spoke about discrimination. The Catholic woman spoke about discrimination. The black woman talked about how she could . . . she could not try on clothes before she bought them. How she could not take a trip with her parents because they couldn't use the restrooms. How she couldn't eat at most places. And of course, seeing these professional women—we had social workers, we had teachers, we had an opera singer, we had various . . . we had a lawyer's wife. So you know they were on the panel. It was very . . . it all led up to then the Protestant woman saying, "Well, I could do whatever I wanted. I don't remember ever having been discriminated against."

> And we spoke to groups all over the state, schools, churches, synagogues, social work organizations . . . just you name it, also a couple of men's groups. The men's groups, the men's luncheon groups were, I think, the hardest groups to talk to. Because they regarded us as, "Well, little lady." You know. "What do you have to tell us?" It was that attitude.

> We also spoke . . . in many schools. They were very welcoming. There were a lot of questions asked of the Jewish panelists. And it was appalling to me at that time how little was known about the Jewish community or about

Judaism within the state. I was really amazed. Today, I don't think you would find that. But at that time it was so little known. It was . . . it was really terrible.

Those were the two things that I think really surprised me was the condescension of the men and the appalling lack of anything about Judaism.

We had a high school in Vicksburg, Mississippi, and . . . it was the first question. "Did you kill Jesus?" Now here she is 16, 17 years old and she is

---

Murder of Three Civil Rights Workers in Mississippi

On June 21, 1964, three civil rights workers left Meridian, Mississippi, for the 50-mile trip to Longdale, Mississippi, to inspect the ruins of Mount Zion United Methodist Church. The church, which had been a meeting place for civil rights groups, had been the target of arson five days earlier. James Chaney (age 21), a black man and a Freedom Movement activist from Meridian, Mississippi; Michael Schwerner (age 24), a Congress of Racial Equality organizer from New York; and Andrew Goodman (age 20), a Freedom Summer volunteer, also from New York, knew that the White Citizens Council and the Ku Klux Klan had taken their license tag as they were leaving Meridian. Although the men had established security procedures with specific check-in times, they were stopped in Neshoba County. The Ku Klux Klan stopped the car and took the three workers to an isolated spot where Chaney was severely beaten and all were shot to death. Their bodies were buried in a dam under construction and their car driven into Bogue Chitto Swamp. A sheriff's deputy and his staff lied when Freedom workers called searching for their missing friends.

The disappearance of these three civil rights workers captured national attention, and President Lyndon B. Johnson ordered the Federal Bureau of Investigation to investigate the case. It took six weeks before the workers' bodies, along with the bodies of seven other Mississippi black activists, were found. President Johnson used the national outrage over this tragedy to move forward with the Civil Rights Act of 1964 as well as the Voting Rights Act of 1965 (*Mississippi Civil Rights Workers Murders*, 2009).

For more than 40 years, the murders of these three young men remained unsolved, and no one was prosecuted for this heinous crime. In recognition of the 40th anniversary of the murders, a multiethnic group of more than 1,500 people issued a call for justice. Under the leadership of the Winter Institute for Racial Reconciliation at the University of Mississippi, named after former Governor William Winter (1980–1984), the people of Neshoba County began to talk about those past events in their community.

In 2005, Edgar Ray Killen, a local minister in Neshoba County, then 80 years of age, was tried and found guilty of three counts of murder. He appealed, and the Mississippi Supreme Court upheld the verdict in 2007. Although much healing still needs to occur in Neshoba County, William Winter has been an outspoken leader and pioneer for improving race relationships in Neshoba County and in Mississippi as a whole (see Broder, 2005).

saying, "Did you kill Jesus?" Especially when we spoke to Baptist groups. . . .
It was like they had never been out of Mississippi. That was the feeling that I
had. If you lived in Mississippi . . . but I always felt that if you are going to live
in Mississippi it was a nice life, but you had to get out. I sent my children away
as much as I possibly could, and the nice part was that . . . the nice part was
that we earned a good living and we were able to do it.

Our temple was bombed in the '60s. Rabbi's house was bombed at the
same time. And it was a very scary time. During this period nearly every civil
rights activist living in Jackson was killed. And the three civil rights young men
who came to Mississippi to help open the state up were killed in Mississippi,
in Philadelphia, Mississippi. Members of the Ku Klux Klan were arrested
and convicted. Jewish men within the Jackson community worked with the
[Federal Bureau of Investigation] to help convict the Ku Klux Klan. Some of
the things . . . that . . . well there was a bombing in Meridian, Mississippi. And
then in 1966 I remember a book was published by a Mississippi writer, James
Silver. And I believe he was a professor at Ole Miss. And I believe the book
was called *Mississippi: The Closed Society*, which summed up what had happened to the state. The economy remained stagnant. Few people moved into
the state, and many others left. It was an exciting time, in that you met a lot
of very interesting people, but it was also a very, very scary time. Leaflets . . .
Ku Klux Klan dropped leaflets at the house calling you Jewish names—Dirty
Jew—or whatever the Ku Klux Klan . . .

In fact in 1965, that's when . . . or '64, '65, that's when they passed the
Civil Rights Act . . . where you could stay at hotels . . . and so my husband
went with us a number of times 'cause here we were, we were going to rent
rooms in the hotel and stay together. And nothing ever happened, but we
did not know. So for a while he went with us. We went to Starkville, we
went to Clarksdale. . . . Because we were invited to by a lot of churches
that time, all over the state. Episcopal churches, Catholic churches, Baptist
churches in Jackson.

Societal/Structural Aspects of Resilience

JG remembered the sociocultural climate of the day:

Civil Rights legislation was enacted in the early '60s. And an innovative
Head Start program was developed for children—3-, 4-, and 5-year-olds and
their parents. Health and nutritional programs for adults were started. This
was a program called the Child Development Group of Mississippi (CDGM).
It was for rural Mississippians . . . poor Mississippians. The closest one to
Jackson was in Canton, Mississippi. But they were in all the small communities within Mississippi. National leaders in the field developed the curriculum

for CDGM. And it was really . . . it was not a kindergarten, it was a total program. This was to bring the parents and have the parents involved. Parents were trained as aides. At one point CDGM had 7,500 children enrolled in the program. I was part of a statewide board. The idea was to have representatives from each community on the state board. And then whites to help develop the idea of running, the leadership for the program, the local leadership. And we had many, many meetings. All our meetings were at least until 12, 1, 2 in the morning because these were people . . . mostly not well educated, who came to the meetings. And they didn't know how to be a cohesive board. And that was the purpose of the whites who were willing to participate in this thing. And we met . . . I was on the board for several years. And we went to some of the programs. I remember going to one in Canton, one in Starkville, I believe, and they were really very innovated. It was not the idea, it was not to teach the children how to learn . . . how to read. It was really to prepare them for school. And there were no kindergartens at that time in Mississippi.

Bombing of Beth Israel Congregation

On September 18, 1967, violence and intimidation was directed toward the Jewish community in Jackson, Mississippi. The Ku Klux Klan bombed Beth Israel Congregation, the city's only Jewish synagogue, which had recently been constructed. Its dedication had taken place only months earlier and had included members of the interfaith and interracial committees, the Greater Jackson Clergy Alliance, and the Council of Human Relations. These organizations were committed to improving social conditions and resolving racial problems in Mississippi.

Rabbi Perry Nussbaum, the leader of the congregation, was straightforward, outspoken, and a social reformer. The bombing of his study occurred a few days after Beth Israel hosted a meeting of the Council on Human Relations. There was an outpouring of support and concern from local clergy of many denominations, including a "walk of penance" to "exhibit our sorrow at what had happened to the Jewish community . . . we decided that the best thing to do would be to express that in public. . . . We expressed our condolences and our determination out of our feelings of guilt at not having been able to lead the community in the direction in which we felt it ought to go," recalled Reverend Tom Tiller, at the 40th anniversary celebration of the bombing (*40th Anniversary of the Bombing of Jackson's Beth Israel Congregation*, 2007). The Ku Klux Klan struck a third time on May 28, 1968, bombing Congregation Beth Israel in Meridian, Mississippi. This streak of violence came to an end when Klan members were finally captured while attempting to bomb the home of Meyer Davidson, an active and a well-respected leader in the Meridian Jewish community (see Appendix).

There were many programs within the state at that point. From [Lyndon B. Johnson's] Great Society there were many programs that were started. The Panel of American Women began in 1965. I saw it with a group of teenagers in Little Rock, Arkansas. It was a youth group. And this was a program that had been started in Kansas City by Esther Brown. . . . It was after 1957, I believe, and she was asked to develop a program for Brotherhood Week. And she developed this. And word . . . and it was so well received that she began to get asked to bring the program to different places. And then other cities began to ask her how to develop a program, this program. So I decided that I thought we could bring it Mississippi.

Markers of Resilience

JG did not grow up dreaming that she would be a social activist and agent of change; yet her narrative demonstrates that disruptions occur in our lives, and often such disturbances occur in a sociocultural and historical context (Becker, 1997). These events may serve as turning points on an individual and community level, reflecting the interdependence between one's life and the larger mutual interplay between self and environment. Carr (1986) explained that this reciprocity of roles occurs because "in the complex actions and experiences of everyday life we are subjects or agents, narrators, and even spectators to the events we live through and the actions we undertake" (p. 64).

JG reflected on her early memories of feeling different:

When I said I was not discriminated against growing up. You know, I remember hearing about the Holocaust. I remember . . . so there were a lot of things that you knew that Jewish people were discriminated against. And I happen to be Jewish.

Another marker of resilience was how JG handled her confrontation with the WCC in Mississippi in the 1950s and 1960s:

So when these White Citizens Council representatives came to the house, I said, no, that I was not interested in joining. And then became aware of racial problems that had never really been . . . I had not been active in the community before that. Only in my own little community. And raising my children. Began to be concerned about what would happen to the community as these things were . . . as questions were coming up. So it was either, the way they phrased it, it was either you join them or you're against them. . . .

And so then I . . . we began to be concerned about the school system. We were afraid the schools would close if they were forced to integrate. The amazing thing is that it never . . . the schools never closed. But that was our initial fear and the fear that pervaded probably all of the 60s.

When I started the panel, I contacted Esther Brown and she was a very dynamic woman who . . . I never knew just how far she was involved in the

1954 Brown versus . . . I'm not sure, but she always indicated that she had something to do with it. But I'm not sure exactly what . . . whether it was named after her or what. But she was very active in Kansas City. And she came to Mississippi. She came to Jackson. We were the first panel that was started in the Deep South. And so she helped us. She helped us develop the script, and she helped us at our meetings. And then afterwards, I went with her . . . met her in Memphis. And we developed a panel in Memphis; we developed a panel in Birmingham. So there were . . . I know there was a panel here in Dallas that was very active also.

We formed the Panel of American Women to go across Mississippi to speak against prejudice, including racism and anti-Semitism. It was well worth it for all children and for me to see my daughter grow up to be a reformer herself.

End-of-Chapter Questions and Activities

1. How does JG enact social and economic justice?
2. What affect do her activities appear to have on her children's lives?
3. Write a brief summary on the founding of Head Start. What social and historical events led to its establishment?

References

40th Anniversary of the Bombing of Jackson's Beth Israel Congregation. (2007, September 1). (Press release issued by Goldring/Woldenberg Institute of Southern Jewish Life, P.O. Box 16528, Jackson, MS 39236-0528)

Barnes, P. C. (2002). Sara Alderman Murphy and the Little Rock Panel of American Women: A prescription to heal the wounds of the Little Rock School Crisis. In R. Finley & T. A. DeBlack (Eds.), *The Southern elite and social change: Essays in honor of Willard B. Gatewood, Jr.* (pp. 164–176). Fayetteville: University of Arkansas Press.

Becker, G. (1997). *Disrupted lives: How people create meaning in a chaotic world.* Berkeley: University of California Press.

Broder, D. S. (2005, January 16). Mississippi healing. *Washington Post*, p. B7.

Carr, D. (1986). *Time, narrative, and history.* Bloomington: Indiana University Press.

Cohen, H. L., Greene, R. R., Lee, J., Gonzalez, J., & Evans, M. (2006). Older adults who overcame oppression. *Families in Society, 87*, 35–42.

July 11, 1954: Citizens Council formed. (n.d.). Retrieved February 10, 2009, from http://www.usm.edu/crdp/html/cd/citizens.htm

Mississippi civil rights workers murders. (2009). Retrieved February 25, 2009, from Wikipedia: http://en.wikipedia.org/wiki/Mississippi_civil_rights_worker_murders

Murphy, S. A. (1997). *Breaking the silence: Little Rock's Women's Emergency Committee to Open Our Schools, 1958–1963.* Fayetteville: University of Arkansas Press.

Panel of American Women records, 1963–1999. (n.d.). Retrieved February 8, 2009, from http://www.cals.lib.ar.us/butlercenter/manuscripts/collection/mss99-25.htm

Sue, D. W. (2006). *Multicultural social work practice.* Hoboken, NJ: John Wiley.

White Citizens' Council. (2009a). Retrieved February 25, 2009, from NationMaster–Encyclopedia: http://www.nationmaster.com/encyclopedia/White-Citizens%27-Council

White Citizens' Council. (2009b). Retrieved February 25, 2009, from Wikipedia: http://en.wikipedia.org/wiki/White_Citizens%27_Council

Wolin, S. J., & Wolin, S. (1993). *The resilient self: How survivors of troubled families rise above adversity.* New York: Villard.

APPENDIX

Press Release

FOR IMMEDIATE RELEASE:

September 1, 2007

FOR INFORMATION CONTACT:

Stuart Rockoff, Historian, Goldring/Woldenberg Institute
601-362-6357 / rockoff@isjl.org
Valerie Cohen, Rabbi, Beth Israel Congregation
601-956-6215 / rabbicohen@bellsouth.net

40th Anniversary of the Bombing of Jackson's Beth Israel Congregation

Jackson, MS—On September 18, 1967, a shaken Jackson community gathered together to mourn the bombing of Beth Israel Congregation, the city's only Jewish house of worship. On September 18, 2007, Jacksonians will again gather at Beth Israel, this time for a bittersweet program to remember the terror and violence of that time and celebrate the spirit of interfaith cooperation that grew out of this tragic event.

Cosponsored by Beth Israel, the Goldring/Woldenberg Institute of Southern Jewish Life, and the Mississippi Religious Leadership Conference, the event will take place at 7 p.m. at Beth Israel Congregation in Jackson. The Honorable Governor William F. Winter will give the keynote address in a program of reflection and prayer. The Reverend Hosea Hines and Bishop Joseph Latino will also participate.

Early in the night of September 18, 1967, several Ku Klux Klan members detonated a powerful bomb outside the rabbi's study in Beth Israel's brand new synagogue. Just months earlier, Rabbi Perry Nussbaum, the congregation's progressive and outspoken leader, had dedicated the new synagogue in an interfaith, interracial ceremony. Many of Jackson's leading clerics participated in this event as they were friends of Nussbaum's and fellow leaders in civil rights causes and organizations.

Rabbi Nussbaum was an active member of the Greater Jackson Clergy Alliance and Council on Human Relations, both interfaith, interracial committees working to improve the social problems of Mississippi. That the temple was bombed just days after Beth Israel hosted a meeting of the Council on Human Relations confirmed for many that the rabbi's civil rights involvement provoked the attack.

These same Jackson-area clerics convened three days after the bombing of Beth Israel to lead a "Walk of Penance." As Reverend Tom Tiller, the organizer of the walk, recalls: "To exhibit our sorrow at what had happened to the Jewish community . . . we decided that the best thing to do would be to express that in public . . . We expressed our condolences and our determination out of our feelings of guilt at not having been able to lead the community in the direction in which we felt it ought to go."

Despite this public expression of solidarity and good will toward the Jewish community, the Ku Klux Klan struck again, this time bombing Rabbi Nussbaum's home, on November 21, 1967. The same perpetrators later bombed Congregation Beth Israel in Meridian on May 28, 1968. When they tried to bomb the home of Jewish community leader Meyer Davidson in Meridian, they were captured by authorities thanks to a tip from a Klan informant.

Forty years after these bombings, the Jackson Jewish community is more committed than ever to pursuing interfaith and interracial activities and asserting that "one's conscience cannot be bombed into silence." Beth Israel leaders and congregants are active participants in many interfaith dialogue partnerships as well as groups like Habitat for Humanity, the Amos interfaith network, and the Mississippi Religious Leadership Conference.

Source: *40th Anniversary of the Bombing of Jackson's Beth Israel Congregation.* (2007, September 1). (Press release issued by Goldring / Woldenberg Institute of Southern Jewish Life, P.O. Box 16528, Jackson, MS 39236-0528)

10
GRASS ROOTS ORGANIZER

Biographical Sketch

PC, whose family migrated to the U.S. from the Middle East, is a Catholic nun with a master's degree in social work. She has spent 25 years of her professional life working in Texas colonias. She is currently working in Dallas, Texas, as a community organizer, bringing people in parishes together to discuss their future aspirations. She has organized groups to improve local schools and hospitals. Her interest is in how power dynamics influence decision making among members of the church as well as communities with whom she works. She also focuses on the multicultural factors that define a community, seeing culture as a source of strength and resilience.

Historical and Socioeconomic Context

Colonia is a Spanish word for an unincorporated neighborhood. In Texas, colonias often lack basic water and sewer systems, paved roads, and safe and sanitary housing (Federal Reserve Bank of Dallas, n.d.). These areas have a limited property tax base and may be in an isolated rural area or outside the city limits. Texas has more colonias than any other state. About 500,000 people live in 2,300 colonias along the Texas–Mexico border.

People living in colonias, most of whom originally migrated from Mexico to find a better economic life, experience many daunting social and economic justice issues. They generally have very low incomes and attend poorly equipped schools, and their homes often lack the basic amenities of electricity and plumbing. The unemployment rate in some colonias is more than eight times the state rate. In addition, work is seasonal with field work representing the largest share of jobs.

Many colonias do not have sewer systems. Where sewer systems exist, many residents cannot afford the hookup fee. Their untreated wastewater discharged directly into the Rio

Texas Colonias: Location, Development, Conditions, and Challenges

Location

There are colonias in several states, including Texas, New Mexico, Arizona, and California. Texas, however, has both the largest number of colonias and the largest colonia population, estimated at 400,000. In Texas alone, there are more than 2,294 colonias, most located along the state's 1,248-mile Mexican border. About 65 percent of the colonia population is Hispanic; 85 percent of all colonia residents under 18 were born in the United States.

Development

Colonias in Texas were developed circa the 1950s from land that was useless for agriculture, worthless, and/or lay in floodplains. By dividing land into small plots, developers created unincorporated subdivisions. There was little or no investment in infrastructure, and the lots were then sold to low-income individuals in need of affordable housing. The incomes of colonia residents are generally quite low, and per capita annual incomes in all Texas counties along the Mexico border tend to be significantly below the state average of $16,717. In 1994, Starr, Maverick, and Hidalgo Counties' per capita annual incomes were $5,559, $7,631, and $8,899, respectively.

Why People Buy Land in Colonias

New colonias are developed and existing ones expanded because there is a limited supply of adequate, affordable housing in both urban and rural areas on the Texas–Mexico border. With expanding need for such housing, people with low incomes have tended to buy lots through a contract for deed—a method of property financing that features low down payments and monthly payments but no title to a property until the final payment on it has been made. Because of their limited resources, buyers generally construct houses in phases—adding on as they can afford materials—and the properties may lack electricity, plumbing, and other basic amenities.

Improving Conditions in the Colonias

As colonias continue to grow, residents and the county, state, and federal governments are faced with the challenge of providing basic water and sewer services as well as improving general quality of life. Existing resources, including local public funds, are limited and often inadequate to keep pace with demands for services to the growing colonias populations. An example is Hidalgo County, which has the most colonias and largest number of Texas colonia residents. There, it is typical for residents to rely for basic health and human services, environmental services, and capital improvements on an often confusing patchwork of local, state, and federal programs, many of which appear and disappear with changes in the political and economic climate.

Issues and Challenges

Water and Sewage

One of the greatest concerns in the colonias is the lack of wastewater infrastructure and drinkable water. This has potentially serious negative consequences for public health quality of life in general.

Because many colonias lack sewer systems, residents are forced to rely on alternative, often inadequate waste disposal methods. Septic systems are problematic if too small or improperly installed, and they can overflow. Owing to inadequate drainage systems and the elevation and topography of the colonias, water collects during heavy rains, a condition that in combination with inadequate septic tanks can result in pooling of sewage on the ground. The poor quality of roads in the colonias—they are frequently unpaved and covered with caliche or other materials that impede drainage—makes the problem worse.

Beyond the inadequate sewer systems, colonias lacks adequate wastewater treatment facilities. In many areas, treatment facilities are wholly absent, and as a result, communities frequently dump untreated or inadequately treated wastewater into canals and *arroyos* (creeks or streams) that ultimately feed into the Rio Grande River or the Gulf of Mexico.

It is a challenge for colonia residents to secure drinkable water. They may resort to buying water by the bucket or drum to meet their daily needs, or they may use wells that could be contaminated. Residents often find themselves in a double-bind—unable to access services because their homes do not meet county building codes even where adequate water lines and sewage systems are in place. Many houses have been built without indoor bathrooms or plumbing, and housing inspectors will designate these as "substandard" or "dilapidated," so the houses cannot pass inspection to qualify for hookup to water lines *and* residents are unable to afford the repairs or improvements necessary to bring them up to code.

Housing

As mentioned, colonias residents tend to construct housing in a piecemeal fashion, using whatever materials are available and that they can afford. Use of professional building services is rare. They frequently begin with tents or temporary wood or cardboard structures and, as finances allow, continue to build and make improvements to their homes. Housing in the older colonias, where residents have had more time to make improvements, is generally better developed.

Health

Disease is common and tends to proliferate in colonias because of dilapidated housing conditions, a lack of safe drinking water and adequate sewer and drainage systems, and floodplain locations. According to the Texas Department of Health data, rates of

In another example of hope, PC described her mother's resilience and decision to live and function within her family:

My mother is 86 years old, and my dad died eight years ago when she was 78. She had never, ever, ever lived by herself from . . . she had just never lived by herself. When he died, then she lived by herself. None of us lived in Alexander, which is where we grew up. And then two years after my dad died she became deathly ill. She basically had to make a decision if she was going to live or die. I was visiting her in the hospital and she said, "Am I going to die?" and I said, "Do you want to die?" And she said, "No, I don't." She said, "I want to spend more time with" (there are four of us in the family) "the four of you. I have not spent as much time with you as I've wanted to." She said, "I don't want to die," and I said, "Well, then you're not going to die." And she's still living. But when you said connected to something larger you're right, there is something, there has to be strength within you but there has to be a connection outside that you see yourself a part of. If you don't have that, then no matter how much strength you have internally, it's going to wear down.

Interpersonal Aspects of Resilience

PC does not believe that unilateral power is the way to community change. Rather, she suggested that power is relational and that communities can only be organized through mutual consent:

Most of us have only experienced unilateral power, which is just power over someone. "I do for you and/or I do to you." In relational power, there is a mutual change. This is the listening that we were talking about. The community organizer thinks about what kind of action the other person needs to take. I think that's really the core of the change process. [That is,] having enough self-awareness to be very careful about that boundary between you and the client.

One of my favorite authors talked about education being about teaching power. He discusses how to develop consent. You don't want to coerce, persuade, give misinformation, or propaganda. The best way that you get consent is by developing [another person's] judgment. It's only in that way that education leads then that both people change and that you can develop real power.

Sociocultural Aspects of Resilience

Interviewer: So what's the power of change and community building?

PC: The power is, oh gosh, several things. One is being able to change in a small way, but being able to change the way the world is or the way the dominant culture is. The dominant culture teaches us that we are only to be among our own. My grandparents came from Syria, so . . . the dominant culture suggests to only associate with Arabs. Don't cross lines, or if you do cross lines you be very cautious about how you do that.

In our [community-building] organizations, we cross, we go counter to all of that. We have Muslims, Jews, Christians, Catholics, and Protestants. We have . . . white upper-middle class, probably maybe a couple wealthy, but mostly upper-middle class. We have lower class, we have recent immigrants. If you come to a meeting we have to have translation equipment. So the power is [that] it goes counter to what the dominant culture says. In that way, it goes counter to who can make a change.

Societal/Structural Aspects of Resilience

PC reflected on how connection with community organizing within the Catholic church gives people a sense of resilience or hope that change can happen. She said that they do not have to riot to obtain rights.

Interviewer: Could I ask a question? . . . Would you agree that the religious infrastructure then is part of that macroscene that gives some empowerment that this organization is behind me?

PC: That's right, that's right. For example, I think it was back in the '80s, no '70s, '70s to '80s, there was a big, not just riot, I can't even remember the circumstances in Los Angeles where a whole community just rose up. And I was in San Antonio at the time and I was working in a Catholic congregate parish there and that congregation was connected to COPS, the community organization. And I asked one of the women, "Why haven't y'all done this? Why haven't y'all just risen up and burned and slashed?" And she said, "We don't have to do that because we have an organization where we know if we hang in and stay here long enough change will happen. We're not at a point, it doesn't, it's not just, and we know it's going to happen so there is just no need for us to riot."

That statement gave me a real insight into the work and into what people attach, if you will, their hope to. And it's a question, ya know, I'll wait in line if I see the line moving, but if I don't see that line moving then I'm either going to get out of line or I'm going to not just organize, I'm going to protest, I'm going to burn. But I'm going to do something different if I don't see that line moving.

Because the presence or absence of power is systemic as well as individual, it is a key element in shaping human functioning. "There are some individuals or groups whose exposure to negative valuations have been so intense that they accept these valuations as 'right' " (Solomon, 1976, p. 23). However, controlling one's destiny to some reasonable extent is key to empowerment (Pinderhughes, 1989).

PC believes in a form of community organizing that does not make people dependent or victims. She said, "The worse thing we can do is to do things for people." She also advised that anger be channeled into action.

> PC: I was talking to one of our leaders, who is an immigrant from Honduras. She's (LG) going to a community college to learn English better and she is very smart. Very smart. But she cleans house for a woman in Highland Park, she has two children and she has a husband . . . point of the story, last year after school, we met her through her congregation which is the cathedral downtown. Then she wanted us to organize with her at her school, so we did. We organized a large assembly of parents, we had 400 parents there, and they met with the area superintendent and the principal.
>
> They talked to the superintendent about the changes they wanted in their school. It was real simple, it was safety in terms of traffic patterns and more space for parking. Because their school, which is not unusual in Dallas, was built for 350 students, it has 1,100 students. It has all these portables. Well, you can do it but they don't build the infrastructure. Infrastructure meaning parking, cafeteria, because they still have a cafeteria for 350 kids, library, and bathrooms. So they were able, these parents, were able to get in a whole building just for bathrooms, that was done. The parking is being done and the cafeteria is still being done. Well, part of the cafeteria was not just a space, but how their kids were being treated and how they were being served the food and all that stuff.
>
> The principal decided he didn't want the parents organized. Well, LG kept organizing. And we worked with her, so we got her a meeting with the area superintendent with some parents. So, she's still organizing. . . . This morning . . . she had organized with the area superintendent to have the . . . director of cafeterias of all the district be there to meet with the parents. Well the principal preempted her and had the meeting this morning with 10 parents. She was furious, she called me to tell me. So, she tells me, "He doesn't treat us like

we know what we are doing." She said, "Our agreement was that I can organize the parents to go in with the director of cafeterias, but instead the principal wanted us to go in as individuals." And that's what these 10 parents did. "So everyone went in and was just complaining, but it wasn't organized. It seemed that we did not know what we wanted."

LG said, "I want them to be looked on as competent people who have an agenda, who know what they want, and who can deliver." And she said that's what made her so furious. She said, "He thinks he has to do everything for us. He doesn't respect that we know how to do things for ourselves." I said, "Well then you get some parents together and go tell him that." And she said, "I am, and I'm going to tell the principal that too. You're telling parents they are responsible for their children, you need their help in the schools, but then you treat them as if they are incompetent."

Interviewer: They were splintered [in their power] and sent away. But LG emerged as a local organization, as the leader.

PC: Yes, as the leader. LG said, "This makes me so angry that we were treated like this. No respect." And she said, "Just because we can't speak English doesn't mean we don't know what's happening."

Interviewer: We've heard anger is a mobilizing force. It's a good way to have it channeled so that it makes for change rather than riot, as you said earlier.

PC: Yes, in the [community organizing] training that we do with leaders, this is the first characteristic, and the first quality of a leader is anger. Meaning that you look at things and you are angry . . . at the situation in terms of wanting to change it, in understanding and then having the anger to sustain yourself in changing it. We make a distinction between violence, which is also anger, and depression, which is anger turned in on yourself.

When people have power then they can channel their anger. Violence is anger that is impotent. Depression is anger that is impotent. Alcoholics are angry people because they don't know what to do. They don't have the power to channel their anger, but all of us have anger. We just don't have the power to direct it, to channel.

Interviewer: I'm thinking about [master's in social work] students. How do you teach students . . . not to be afraid of anger? To be able to listen to the anger, because in order to come up with a strategy, you have to step past the anger. You have to transcend that anger, and then go back and then figure the strategies and pick up that anger so that you've got the two of them. That there's a transcendence of the anger.

PC: That's right. The anger has to be taken into a strategy, into an action. Otherwise, it'll go the other directions. Into either depression and turned in on yourself or just unbridled.

Interviewer: Yes, you are teaching me what it means that somebody gets beyond anger.

Markers of Resilience

Attending to real, systemic factors is central to social work practice, especially among people who are combating poverty and disenfranchisement. Therefore, social services, in this case community development interventions, must be structured accordingly (Pinderhughes, 1989). PC expressed her own views of community organizing and how to teach students.

Interviewer: Where do you get started? I heard you say you did your work, and it must be awfully hard to leave as you see this great progress and you move to a new place. What is a beginning for you? Say you arrive here in Dallas, where do you begin?

PC: Well, when I came here every place you go there is an organization, now there is. When I was in San Antonio I put one of those organizations together, but there is always a group that you move into or with. For example, in San Antonio when I put that organization together, there were eight pastors that wanted this type of organization in that community, so I started with them. And perhaps, anyway I started with them and they connected me and told me who to talk to within their congregation and also among other congregations.

PC meets with people of the colonias as individuals, one by one, recognizing that they may not want to make a personal statement in public or risk being embarrassed by talking about their aspirations for change in front of family and friends (Garcia & Van Soest, 2006):

So over a two-year period there I did 1,000 individual meetings talking to people about what their interests were, what were their dreams, what were their visions, what were their passions. What did they want to do in their community, what kind of change did they want to see. And my experience in this work is that people, nobody talks to each other about things like that. They just don't, and because we don't talk to each other about those kinds of pieces of ourselves, then people become passive, they become clients, they become—it's worse than customers—they become very passive and there's a learned—they don't just they become victims—a real learned helplessness. And so then people, you can go all into the self-esteem piece, but the more important piece is, they're victims so they don't think they can do anything. And so, at that point there is no hope because I'm not capable of doing anything different than the way I'm being perceived.

"Oppression is defined as a situation in which one segment of the population acts to prevent another segment from attaining access to resources or acts to inhibit or devalue and dominate them" (Garcia & Van Soest, 2006, p. 70). PC is aware that people who are oppressed come to see their problems as personal deficits rather than society's oppressive nature (Goldenberg, 1978). Therefore, empowerment involves the practitioner's belief in the idea that community members will develop the capacity to change themselves and their environment.

Interviewer: Okay, we're hoping students will learn from this in terms of practice methods. So, it isn't frightening to listen to 1,000 people's dreams and passions and wonder if you can deliver?

PC: No, I don't deliver. They deliver.

Interviewer: That's it. Okay.

PC: They deliver.

Interviewer: But see, I think that's exactly the student question because when they are doing more clinical, one-to-one work they have the fantasy they can deliver. But if you're there listening to hundreds, then thousands of people all saying, "I want something," wow, I can't deliver.

PC: Exactly.

Interviewer: So, it mobilizes them to begin thinking of themselves not as a victim and this is really the process of community building that you described.

PC: That's right, because then what you do, I did 1,000, 2,000 meetings, then we brought the key leaders together. And that ended up being, the first meeting we had about 400. And then that eventually became 200. And they became the core of the organization, which then when we launched it, we launched with 1,000 people again. But it was that group of 200 in the different institutions that talked to each other, what they talked about, what their dreams, what their hopes, passions were. And then they take the responsibility.

There is a growing body of literature that views resiliency as a phenomenon that involves meaning making, growth, and transformation following adversity (Janoff-Bulman, 1992; Saleebey, 2008).

PC described how hope and religious connections can foster resilience:

> So the hope then comes both from the religious institution they are connected to and seeing that change can happen and it is happening. When I left that parish they gave me a farewell, what they call a *despeidida*, and one of the women got up and said, this is the religious connection, they had been going to Bible studies at the same time that we were organizing and in the Bible study they had studied the Exodus. And she said she didn't understand what the Exodus meant until she became involved in the organizing experience, because what the Exodus began to mean for her was leaving behind the poor housing, the poor education, and moving into—creating a new life and new land for them was the better housing. More importantly, being able to connect to and speak to and engage with city council and having city council listen to them. And to them that was the Exodus from where they were and then that . . .

Interviewer: That's a powerful metaphor.

PC: Well it was, and they taught me much more than I taught them in that situation, I have to say. And so when I talk about the hope, I think that also gave them the hope when they could see what changes they could bring about, what relationships and connections they could make within the community, with each other and then sustain that over a period of time.

Finally, PC's form of community organizing emphasizes the positive contribution of diversity to the progress of the group:

> For example, here in Dallas we just had a meeting of the organization. We had 30 people. And we started the meeting by doing what we call individual meetings, where they talk to each other about why they are there and what they wanted. Well, we had a guy—I know he's very wealthy, talking to a woman who is African American, and relatively low income. He's white. So they're talking about what their dreams and passions are. So afterwards we ask people what did you learn and he said, "I learned that Tonya and I have the same hopes. We both want our grandchildren to go to college and to be well educated and to be successful."
>
> Well, you start breaking down those barriers and people start to understand they have common interests. They then start saying, "What do we need to do?" Or we agitate them toward, what do you have to do then to see that your grandchildren, no matter where you live in Dallas, are going to be able to go to college?

And then when you say it's overwhelming, it's not because they put it together. The other we did last night, we had already put together a recent action research team around health care and around keeping the hospital. And that's going to be mammoth; in fact, someone told us to stay out—it's too big of an issue.

End-of-Chapter Questions and Activities

1. What was PC's philosophy of community development? How did this philosophy contribute to individual and community resilience?
2. Choose a community in your state that has a high rate of poverty and poor housing. Write a two-page concept paper presenting the data and outlining a community organization plan. What would be your constituency groups?

References

Federal Reserve Bank of Dallas. (n.d.). *Texas colonias: A thumbnail sketch of the conditions, issues, challenges and opportunities*. Retrieved February 10, 2009, from http://www.dallasfed.org/ca/pubs/colonias.html

Garcia, B., & Van Soest, D. (2006). *Social work practice for social justice*. Alexandria, VA: Council on Social Work Education.

Goldenberg, I. I. (1978). *Oppression and social intervention*. Chicago: Nelson-Hall.

Janoff-Bulman, R. (1992). *Shattered assumptions: Toward a new psychology of trauma*. New York: Free Press.

Pinderhughes, E. (1989). *Understanding race, ethnicity, and power*. New York: Free Press.

Saleebey, D. (2008). *The strengths perspective in social work practices* (5th ed.). Boston: Allyn & Bacon.

Solomon, B. (1976). *Black empowerment*. New York: Columbia University Press.

CONCLUSION

NARRATIVE AS TRANSFORMATION

The purpose of narrative gerontology is to give the "listener" insights about the aging process that would not ordinarily be available without hearing the life stories of older adults (Kenyon & Randall, 2001). In this text, we have learned about the resilience of older adults who have lived through challenging historical events and faced social and economic injustices in the societal/structural, sociocultural, interpersonal, and personal aspects of their lives (see Table 6). Thus, the personal stories presented in this volume give the reader the opportunity to witness events that bridge individual and social change. They give us a deeper understanding of the oppression of their day, and teach us about the feelings and thoughts that allowed them to become social workers, educators, and social activists.

When we review the structural dimensions of their stories, we can better understand how individuals can influence and change the very institutions of a society (Goldenberg, 1978). For example, AS and the admissions officer of the University of Texas School of Social Work ignored the governor's order that "no African Americans will attend the University of Texas." JG turned down the White Citizens Council who sought her support for their segregationist cause; and the descendants of Quakertown mobilized to get a senior center built in their neighborhood.

An examination of the stories also allows us to see "how times have changed." Our storytellers lived at a time when they did not have access to public facilities. JM recalled being "persuaded" to sit at the back of the bus; descendants of Quakertown remembered having to sit in the theater balcony and having to eat their ice cream cone outdoors rather than at the ice cream counter; and black parents often taught their children not to drink at the "white" water fountain.

In addition, stories illustrated community resilience as storytellers recalled the support of family and neighbors. JS believed that the retention of his culture and language of origin was important to family resilience in his new country. Several families attributed their strength to their religious faith. The personal optimism and hope of our storytellers is exemplified by their willingness to help others. PC dedicated her life to helping people living in the colonias; GG worked to increase educational opportunities in his state.

Social Work Practice Implications

Client stories are unique and are composed of a mixture of pain, hope, and pride (Hallberg, 2001). A narrative may be used to facilitate a therapeutic conversation that allows clients to rewrite their story, giving new meaning to their life events (see Gergen, 1985). This in turn may lend itself to a more positive meaning of an adverse event (Greene, 2008). According to Updergraff and Taylor (2000), this may help improve a client's self-concept, increasing his or her appreciation of relationships, and enhancing personal growth.

The lessons learned from the storytellers also suggest that social work practice with older adults should take into account their challenges and accomplishments throughout the life course. Their lives are more than a series of events. Rather, events as recounted in the story usually form an integrated and coherent self (Butler, 1968).

Life span development can best be understood from this vantage point (Shaw, 2001) and this can open up ideas for social work practice. The narrative form of intervention can provide opportunities for a client to forge new meanings of events, discover a newfound sense of integrity, and achieve psychological and spiritual integration and healing. This idea is best captured by Robert Butler, the father of life review therapy, foreshadowing a resilience approach to old age. He said that the psychotherapy of old age is

> coming to terms with, bearing witness, reconciliation, atonement, construction and reconstruction, integration, transcendence, creativity, realistic insight with modifications and substitutions, the introduction of meaning and of meaningful, useful, and contributory efforts: these are the terms that are pertinent to therapy with older people. (p. 237)

References

Butler, R. N. (1968). Toward psychiatry of the life-cycle: Implications of sociopsychologic studies of the aging process for the psychotherapeutic situation. In A. Simon & L.L. Epstein (Eds.), *Aging and modern society* (pp. 233–248). Washington, DC: American Psychiatric Press.

Cohen, H., Greene, R. R., Gonzalez, J., Lee, Y., & Evans, M. (2005). Older adults who overcame oppression. *Families in Society, 87*(1), 1–8.

Gergen, K. J. (1985). The social construction movement in modern psychology. *American Psychologist, 40,* 266–275.

Goldenberg, I. I. (1978). *Oppression and social intervention.* Chicago: Nelson-Hall.

Greene, R. R. (2008). *Social work practice: A risk and resilience perspective.* Monterey, CA: Thomson Brooks/Cole.

Hallberg, I. (2001, March 27–30). *Caring for and being cared for: Nurses, families and the person with Alzheimer's disease trying to make sense of a difficult life situation.* National Conference of the Alzheimer's Association Conference Proceedings.

Kenyon, G. M., & Randall, W. L. (2001). Narrative gerontology: An overview. In G. M. Kenyon, P. Clark, & B. de Vries (Eds.), *Narrative gerontology: Theory, research, and practice* (pp. 3–8). New York: Springer..

Shaw, M.E. (2001). A history of guided autobiography. In G. M. Kenyon, P. Clark, & B. de Vries (Eds.), *Narrative gerontology: Theory, research, and practice* (pp. 291–309). New York: Springer.

Updegraff, J.A., & Taylor, S.E. (2000). From vulnerability to growth: Positive and negative effects of stressful life events. In J.H. Harvey & E.D. Miller (Eds.), *Loss and trauma: General and close relationship perspectives* (pp. 3–28). Philadelphia, PA: Brunner-Routledge.

Table 6: Characteristics of Resilience as Revealed in the Stories of Older Adults: Four Narrative Dimensions

I. **Structural dimension,** encompassing social policies, power relations, and economic conditions
   ❖ obtaining resources such as housing, water, and sewage
   ❖ accessing education and health care
   ❖ using transportation and recreational facilities
   ❖ obtaining economic security through equal employment and job opportunity
   ❖ establishing and influencing institutional and community structures such as banking, and professional and volunteer organizations
   ❖ participating in national movements such as the civil rights movement
   ❖ advocating for equality and combating oppressions such as racism, anti-Semitism, and sexism
   ❖ realigning power differentials

II. **Sociocultural dimension,** referring to social meaning associated with aging and the life course
   ❖ learning from one's culture of origin
   ❖ creating coalitions
   ❖ developing and advocating for a community vision
   ❖ combating oppressive conditions
   ❖ affirming positive past events and behaviors
   ❖ contrasting other generations

III. **Interpersonal dimension,** including family and friends
   ❖ mentoring others to succeed
   ❖ teaching in your community to achieve aspirations
   ❖ leading others in a cause
   ❖ providing unconditional love
   ❖ learning about others' cultures
   ❖ giving family and community support
   ❖ playing and working with peers
   ❖ forming activist groups
   ❖ creating a safe and secure environment

IV. Personal dimensions, involving internal meaning and coherence

❖ aspiring to a "better" human condition
❖ achieving one's personal goals
❖ feeling competence under difficult conditions
❖ being able to trust others
❖ hoping for a "bright" future
❖ maintaining one's dignity when oppressed
❖ working for a "better" world
❖ exhibiting strengths such as perseverance and determination
❖ transcending adverse events through spirituality

Source: Adapted with permission from Cohen, H., Greene, R. R., Gonzalez, J., Lee, Y., & Evans, M. (2005). Older adults who overcame oppression. *Families in Society, 87*(1), 1–8.

INDEX